BUGATTI BLUE

PRESCOTT AND THE SPIRIT OF BUGATTI

Dedicated to Rembrandt Bugatti and his works

Also by the author (nonfiction)

The Classic Car Adventure

VC10 Icon of the Skies

Secret Wings of World War II

Secrets of the Spitfire

Spitfire MkV and Variants

Allard The Complete Story

Saab Cars The Complete Story

Saab 99 & 900 The Complete Story

Citroen The Complete Story

Vickers VC10

Heavies

Long Haul

Jetliners

The New Illustrated Encyclopaedia of the Automobile

BUGATTI BLUE

PRESCOTT AND THE SPIRIT OF BUGATTI

PHOTOGRAPHED & WRITTEN BY LANCE COLE
Additional photography by Tim Read

PEN & SWORD
TRANSPORT
AN IMPRINT OF PEN & SWORD BOOKS LTD.
YORKSHIRE – PHILADELPHIA

First published in Great Britain in 2018 by
Pen and Sword Transport
An imprint of
Pen & Sword Books Ltd
Yorkshire - Philadelphia

ISBN 978 1 526 73475 4

A CIP catalogue record for this book is available from the British Library.

Typeset by Aura Technology and Software Services, India.

Printed and bound in India by Replika Pvt. Ltd.

Pen & Sword Books Ltd incorporates the Imprints of Pen & Sword Books Archaeology, Atlas, Aviation, Battleground, Discovery, Family History, History, Maritime, Military, Naval, Politics, Railways, Select, Transport, True Crime, Fiction, Frontline Books, Leo Cooper, Praetorian Press, Seaforth Publishing, Wharncliffe and White Owl.

For a complete list of Pen & Sword titles please contact

PEN & SWORD BOOKS LIMITED
47 Church Street, Barnsley, South Yorkshire, S70 2AS, England
E-mail: enquiries@pen-and-sword.co.uk
Website: www.pen-and-sword.co.uk

Or

PEN AND SWORD BOOKS
1950 Lawrence Rd, Havertown, PA 19083, USA
E-mail: Uspen-and-sword@casematepublishers.com
Website: www.penandswordbooks.com

Contents

Acknowledgements

This book could not have been realised without the help of the Bugatti Owners Club (BOC), The Bugatti Trust, and the men and women of Prescott – owners, drivers, enthusiasts, et al. Edmund Burgess helped me present the idea to the BOC and I am grateful to him. Paul Gibbons, archivist at the BOC, has been key to the telling of facts, and my sincere thanks go to him for all his help and kindness. Thanks to BOC's Charles Trevelyan, and to Chris Rogers, BOC General Manager, and past incumbent Stuart Webster and General Secretary Maggie Webster respectively, who have been of great encouragement, as have been Martin Greenslade and Aline Gallan. John Staveley of *Bugantics* fame is always straight to the point with his enthusiasm and informed opinion, and it is fun to recall Sue Staveley, yet sad to mark her untimely passing, for Sue revelled in Bugatti, the VS-CC vintage cars, marshalling and Prescott and its people; she always solved problems and was always positive. Barrie Price, Stephen Gentry, Mike Preston, Mike Marshall, Julian Eckersley, Roland Duce, Tim Dutton, Mike Bullet, Janet Missen, Ian Patton, Adam Ward all deserve a mention for the donation of time, information and kindness during the preparation of this book. Angela Hucke at The Bugatti Trust has been of great assistance and encouragement as has the Trust itself. Oh, and where would we be without Marshals? Thanks also to the Vintage Sports-Car Club (VS-CC) for accreditation and access over the years. Also, to my mates at the Allard Owners Club – Mike and Diana Knapman, Dave Loveys and all. Thanks to my old friend Tim Read of Perspective Broadcast, with whom I have been photographing and filming for years: some of Tim's photos are found herein alongside my own efforts. All the photographs in this book were taken using Nikon DSLR cameras and Nikon lenses.

Finally, to my wife Anna for all her love and support.

INTRODUCTION

Prescott – The Real Thing

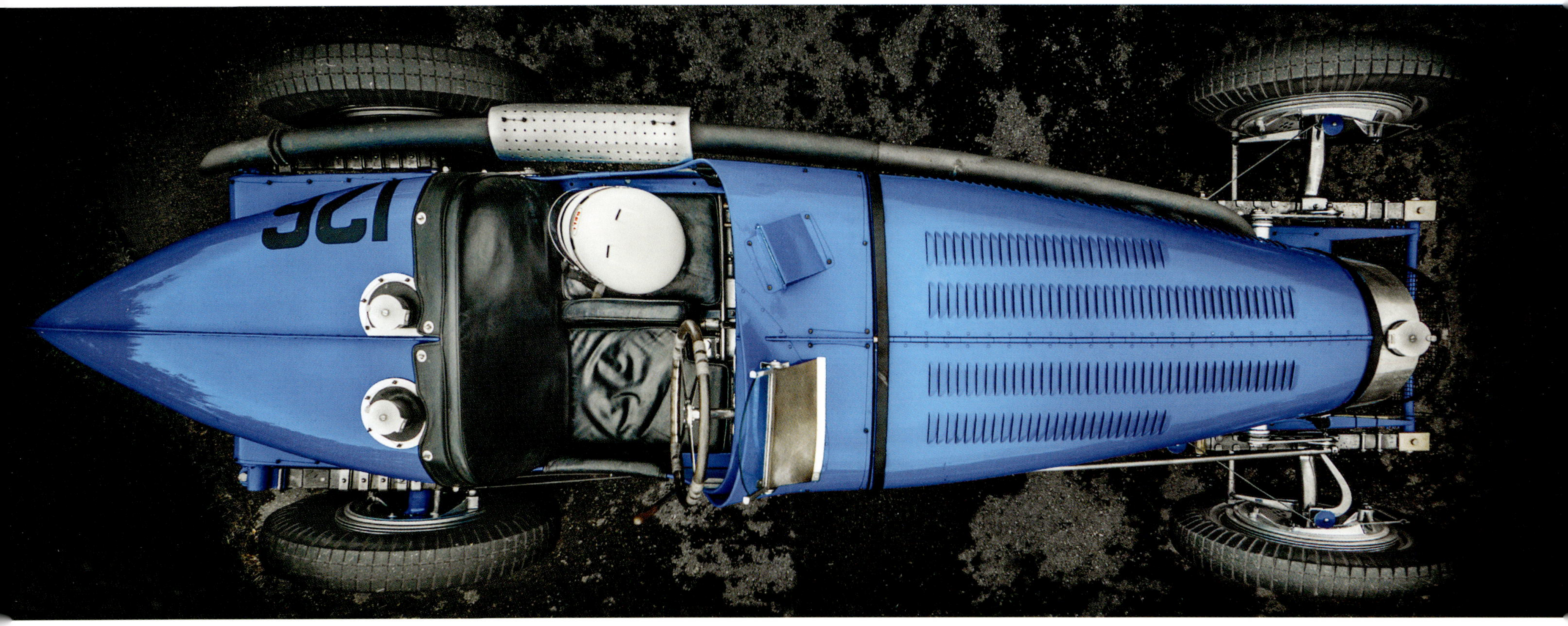

Although it is sometimes said that Prescott is about cars – principally Bugattis, the reality is that Prescott is about people, as well as their cars. Prescott is home to classic Bugatti metal, but also to Edwardian and 1920s-30s mechanical magic of vintage sporting character and their clan of owners. There is a definite aura at Prescott, a real atmosphere, one that is tangible and, on occasions, of real emotion. Here, on a delightful hillside that has seen mechanical motoring action for many decades, can be found something special; a camaraderie that knows no social limits nor status restrictions. In this book, I have attempted to capture that atmosphere – one that has entranced me, and others, for so long.

With whirring crankshafts, popping valves, howling superchargers, wailing induction, and the magic of magnetos, here we find a vintage home for the classic car obsession. As blue hues flash by, as fuel and oil vapours mix, as beer and brandy swill, as men and women laugh and share a unique experience, Prescott really does live. I suppose we must not get too esoteric, but Prescott, its Bugatti story, and the chapters of veteran and vintage classic motoring that accompany it, must rank as something special indeed set against a modern world of marketing, 'celeb' culture and egotism: Prescott is *none* of these, for Prescott and its Bugattis are the real thing. Bugatti, its blue, and that badge that captures it all and which some call the 'Ovale Rouge',

A different angle on Bugatti starts here.

really does come to life on this English hillside. Molsheim's masterpieces seem to love it at Prescott.

Perceived wisdom has it that the Bugatti enthusiasm is an elitist Franco-Italian orientated passion populated by rich people. This may occasionally be true and buying or owning a Bugatti, old or new, does not come cheap. And people, rich or not, tend to spend their money on their Bugattis. However, there is more to Bugatti and to being a Bugatti owner than meets the eye of the conditioned expectation. Not everyone who runs a Bugatti is super-rich; the passion runs deep across all ranks of society. People of many differing personalities and interests share the passion of and for Bugatti, at Prescott.

At Prescott you can be rich or poor, or somewhere in between and you might never know that the person you are talking to is worth millions, because they do not need to tell you; they are there for the cars and the experience, not the ego trip.

The British, in particular, have had an affair with Bugatti since the marque's early days and enjoy a remarkably close association with all things Bugatti. That hillside near the small village of Gotherington in south-west England hosts both the Bugatti Owners Club, and The Bugatti Trust. Both bodies reside at a famous place – Prescott Hill – or more accurately, Prescott Hill Climb. Since 1938, this magical venue has hosted the Bugatti Owners

Club – itself first conceived of in 1929. Bugatti owners, enthusiasts and addicts have travelled from all over the world to this shrine for decades. It is a special place with what today's young would call a 'unique vibe'. Maybe it is the leylines that run through the place, or the ancient standing stones named Odo and Dodo that once stood in the grounds of Prescott House, but Prescott has a real 'feel', a tangible effect upon the person. Odo and Dodo, by the way, were the men who founded nearby Tewkesbury Abbey (we presume they gave their names to the two standing stones), so maybe it is apt that people come to Prescott to worship old cars.

Prescott remains open to all, cheap to access and offers real action right up close to the cars for everyone. Unlike certain venues, it has not created 'enhanced' ticket prices, VIP zones, closed off areas, or elitist enclaves where money and egos run riot. Prescott *remains* to be about people and cars – principally Bugatti cars and vintage cars that you can see, smell and actually touch, whoever you are, whatever your origins or resources. It is people that are key to Prescott, be they drivers, marshals, or spectators; there is a wonderful camaraderie at Prescott; whether you are a billionaire or a builder, it's the passion for the cars that counts.

Prescott provides Bugatti fans with the best days out to be had – probably the best, most open events anywhere in the old car calendar. Through the Bugatti Owners Club, Bugattistes, the Bugatti Trust, and the Vintage Sports-Car Club (VS-CC), we have wonderful events that Prescott hosts. Add in the evocative '*La Vie en Bleu*' weekends, VS-CC gatherings, and you have a nuclei of Bugatti and motor car experiences that offer a visceral, real, sometimes esoteric, but always gripping collection of experiences that are second to none.

The sounds, the smells – the wailing of Bugatti engines, the sound of a Scyntilla Vertex magneto, the whiff of the combustion process and of searing exhausts, flashes of bright blue and other blue hues, shimmering alloys and sweating leather, all combine to provide an amazing, timeless experience far beyond fashion, fads, or marketing hype. Drop the baby Brescia into second gear with a wipe of double declutch and the little car snarls and turns into something else. Or grab hold tightly as a supercharged roller-bearing racer pulls you along in a blur of Type 35 supercharged blue. The sensations just keep on coming.

At Prescott, everyone can get up close and personal to the essence of Bugatti, and of other wonderful old cars from an age before mechanical motoring became a digitally driven authoritarianism.

The sheer level of talent that the Bugatti family encapsulated and expressed represents a true 'high' in the history of industrial design as well as in the driving and racing of cars. Ettore and his son Jean can never be over-hyped; they are of genius beyond compare. And if the newer Bugatti that was the Veyron seemed to lack a certain litheness of style, the latest iteration of Bugatti that is the Chiron, truly is an ellipsoid act of Bugatti design that reeks of the marque's past. Chiron encapsulates true Bugatti etymology. Louis would be proud. Rembrandt (Bugatti, not van Rijn) would have loved it, surely?

Bugattis of old handled with real ability, rode well, steered with accuracy and offered highly tuned, exquisitely engineered engines and chassis. Here was a car that was deliberately *designed* and that *drove*, offering a new approach to motoring and to racing. Here were set down the runes, or maybe even the rules, for a future. And in Britain, Bugatti became something truly special – hence the formation of an owners' club.

The Bugatti 'thing' goes worldwide. The last time I was visiting the BOC's offices, a couple of American Bugatti fans turned up – a married couple who dropped by in a rental car. They owned a Bugatti back home and just *had* to visit Prescott in the closed, off season when they were here. The couple were clearly delighted by their visit to a collection of nondescript buildings clinging to a hillside as the bare apple trees dripped rain and the cloud base lowered. But they were at Prescott!

I have been attending events at Prescott for several decades, often camping out in the Orchard, and only wish I could have been there in 1938 to watch the Giles brothers, or famed driver, raconteur (and later a wartime Resistance figure), Jean-Pierre Wimille in the paddock, or seen Jean Bugatti ambling about taking photographs with his Rolleiflex. What of Arthur Baron, or Jack Lemon Burton (latterly a BOC president) and his incongruously named 'Scuderia Lemon Burton'; or to be at Prescott in 1949 to watch Bugattis battle it out, or Sydney Allard win the 1949 British Hill Climb championship in his bizarre but brilliant Steyr-engined Allard. Indeed, Allard had used the tail, cockpit and scuttle from a wrecked Bugatti in the build of his first true 'Allard Special' of 1936. Many say the parts were taken off Earl Howe's Type 51, but recent research suggests the parts came off the ex-Howe Type 43 Bugatti then owned by Dennis Evans – a 'garagiste' competitor based in Wandsworth – very close to Allard's Fulham base and a Prescott regular. ERAs, Allards, Alfas, Delages, Delahayes, Fiats, and so much more, Prescott provides it all.

I freely admit that Prescott has become an addiction, even when the usually benign weather turns nasty and floods my tent or strands my jalopy in the car park in an island of mud. To be fair, the weather is usually very kind, but when it deluges, it really does.

This book is the result of that passion, that call to sup at the holy grail of Bugatti and all things vintage. Amid the flashing blue and whirring and wailing soundtrack, I wanted to capture and convey to those like-minded, the spell that Prescott casts amid these cars. So herein are moments that I hope you will enjoy, vignettes of my – and your – times at Prescott amid the blue, that wonderful blue.

A Brescia Bugatti powers up Prescott Hill

I am indebted to so many friends, their Bugatti antics, and to strangers, amid the world of Prescott, Bugatti, and vintage cars. To the Bugatti Owners Club, The Bugatti Trust and the Vintage Sports-Car Club, I say a massive thank you. Also, sincere thanks and admiration to a cast of characters from which came access to cars and friendship. I hope that this, the first dedicated collection of colour images of Prescott life seen as a book, can do justice to the atmosphere of Prescott, its cars and its people.

Photographing and experiencing Prescott over the last few years has been one of the greatest joys of my life, particularly during some tough times. My old friend Tim Read has contributed two dozen or so of his images to my own herein, Tim being another man entranced by all things Bugatti and blue. So, let's jump in, warm up the oil, check the magnetos, wipe a smudge of oil off the dashboard and engage the drive mechanism. Prescott and images of Bugatti blue await.

Lance Cole
Wiltshire 2018

Edmund Burgess gets a wheel up out of the Esses – as usual...

Above left: Types 40, 13 and 35 speed away from the Bugatti parking terrace.

Above right: The genius of Ettore Bugatti extended from engines to dashboards. This was true blue glory at Prescott on a summer day some time ago.

Right: Under-the-dashboard coaming, piles of Prescott scrutineers stickers add patina.

Mike Preston curves into Prescott in his Type 35 chassis 37147.

CHAPTER ONE

To Prescott

Bugattis came to Prescott during the heady years of the 1930s when Bugatti was bigger in Britain than some now know. The Bugatti Owners Club (BOC) had begun life as an idea back in 1929 in Buckinghamshire under the encouragement of a number of well-heeled Bugatti owners, not least Viscount Curzon – who, after 1929, was better known as a racing driver, British Racing Drivers Club luminary and Bugatti supporter, and as the fifth Earl Howe.

Francis R.H. Curzon, when Earl Howe, lived close to Chalfont St Giles, where Bugattistes were to 'race' their cars. The Earl was a regular customer of Ettore 'Le Patron' Bugatti and we should not forget that when Ettore Bugatti visited his British customers, and when Jean Bugatti latterly brought the 'works' Bugatti cars and mechanics to England for the summer competition campaigns of the 1930s, Ettore, Jean and his men stayed at the Earl's Buckinghamshire home.

A former Royal Navy officer, and Member of Parliament, Earl Howe had been a dedicated Bentley man and in 1929, only one year after taking to motor racing, raced a Bentley 4½ Litre at Le Mans but only completed a limited number of laps of the Sarthe circuit. But Bentleys and the 'Bentley Boys' in their supercharged heavyweights had had their day by 1930; faster, lighter, more efficient racing cars would eclipse them. Earl Howe purchased an Alfa 8C 2300 racer that had been campaigned by Rudolph Caracciola; in the Alfa, Howe won Le Mans in 1931. By this time, the Earl had purchased several Bugattis as road cars and knew that the Bugatti Type 35 and its derivatives could provide the basis of competitive success on racing tracks and up hill climbs. Ettore Bugatti sold the Earl a Type 51 in which he competed at the 1931 Monaco Grand Prix. Howe won the 1938 Grosvenor House Grand Prix at Cape Town in a Type 59. So, Earl Howe went from Bentley to Bugatti. He supported the Bugattis, their marque, the BOC, and Prescott for decades.

In London in 1929, the British Bugatti concessionaires in Brixton Road (run by Colonel W.L. Sorel), and the Bugatti owners and coachbuilders the Giles brothers, were just down the road, based close to Regents Park.

Colonel Godfrey Giles and his brother Eric owned nineteen Bugattis between 1929 and 1948, and if we remember to include the incredible 'geodetic' glazed hardtop that they added to the Type 57S chassis

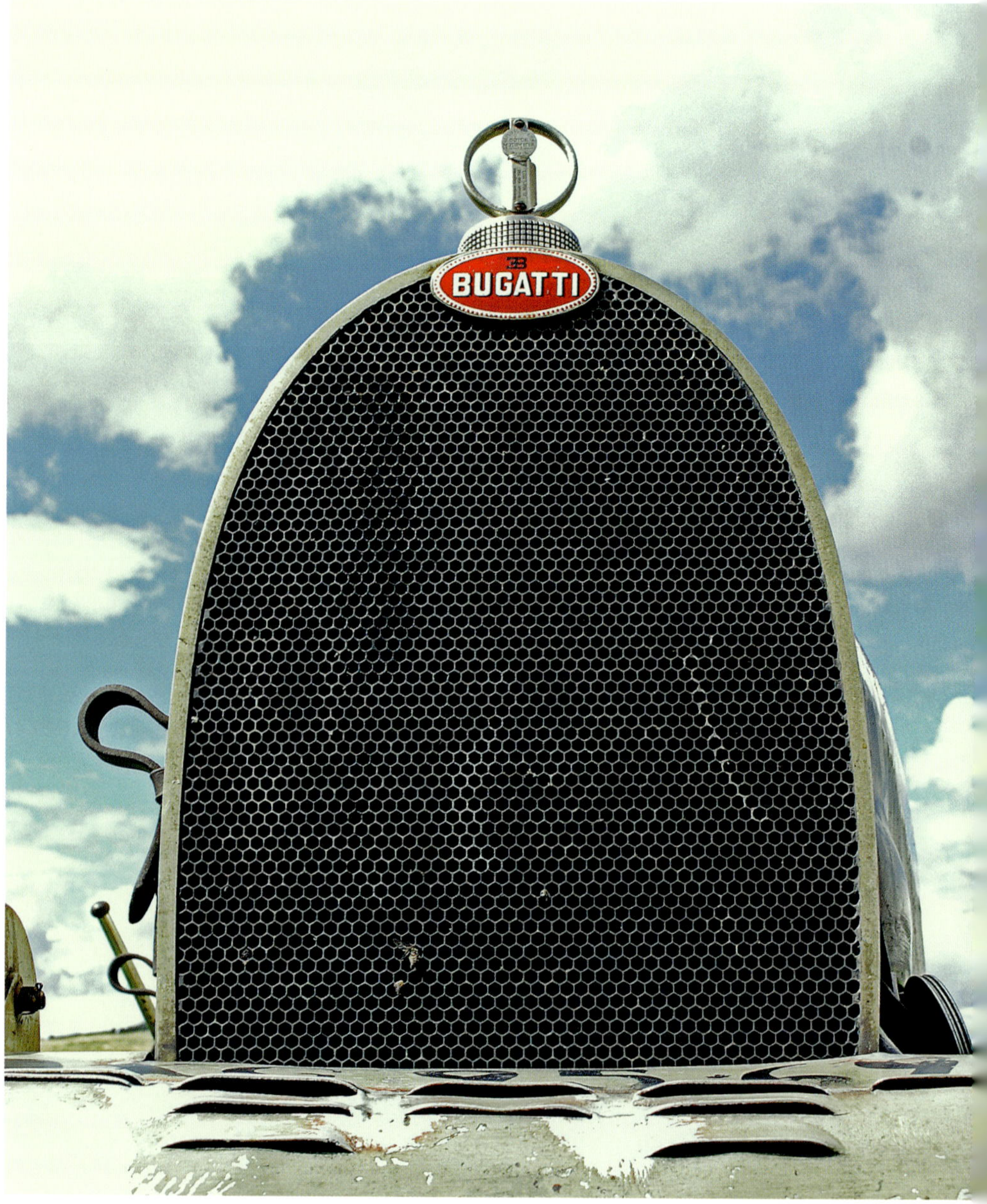

Type 35B (driven by Chris Hudson) and photographed from under the front end to capture the essential Bugatti design motif.

number 57593, the brothers' Bugatti affection became a legend. Given that Eric Giles designed or styled Bugatti bodies that emanated from the Corsica coachworks (and prior to that Bertelli) that were just as elegant as French *carrosserie* coachwork concoctions, we must truly hail the Giles brothers as key to the plot of Bugatti in Britain and at Prescott, where they were closely involved in the site's realisation as a home for Bugatti owners.

The Corsica works (of Corsica Street, prior to a move to Grimaldi Street – keeping a 'continental' theme) bodied several Bugattis and not least, seven of the fifteen Bugatti Type 57s and some owners (such as famed Bugattiste and Prescott stalwart Ronnie Symondson) designed their own car's bespoke, tailored bodies.

No less than Sir Malcolm Campbell 'designed' his own body for his 1937 Type 57S. Campbell's road car, his 'daily driver', was a de-specified Type 35 that made do with a steel body (not alloy), solid front axle (not hollow like the true racers), a non-roller bearing engine (what horror!) and wire wheels instead of hand cast aluminium wheels with their in-built brake housings. It was known as the 'Tecla' – which translates as 'false pearl' – a 'fake' grand prix car then, but not a replica! And it was a pretty fast car around London despite such missing *pur sang* esoterica. Perhaps Campbell's worst 'sin' in purists' eyes was to cut an access hatch in the car's elegant tail and create a boot for his paraphernalia. Ouch!

The Giles brothers were vital to the forming of the Bugatti Owners Club in 1929. Over drinks and cigars in no less an evocative location than Simpson's in the Strand, Godfrey Giles, D.B. Madeley and T. A. Varley came up with the nascent beginnings of a 'Club'. Varley became the first Hon. Secretary, Madeley was the Hon. Treasurer and a Committee (a Council) was formed with Colonel Giles as Chairman. Other early Bugatti Club figures included Kenneth Bear, and Godfrey's brother Eric. Formally framed under the Company's Act, of 1929, the Club became a Limited Company, Incorporated the 22nd day of March 1930. So the Club was formed and the first meeting was held at Colonel Giles' house in Regents Park on 28 March 1930. These events explain the oft-cited but varying dates for the start of the Club; it would be eight years before Bugattis would traverse Prescott's tarmac.

Crucially, the BOC was however now a 1930 reality, albeit homeless. Meanwhile, Ettore Bugatti himself agreed to become the Club's Patron.

The BOC did by 1931 have its own magazine, *Bugantics*, which prospers to this day. Club events were held at Chalfont St Giles and then at Aston Clinton, and they framed the Club's first true gatherings. Shelsley Walsh was by this time the most important British hill climb site having been established as early as 1905. Shelsley would also be the place where Jean Bugatti would badly damage his Type 53 4.9 litre supercharged four-wheel-drive car, effectively ruining his 1932 season.

Mike Bullet and Jakub Stauch speed along – all arms and elbows.

The young BOC needed a permanent home, not least because the locals at Chalfont St Giles started to complain about noise and traffic on their local roads as the competition schedule got busier. The new Club held events at Chalfont, Aston Clinton, Lewes, and at Donington, but it needed a secure base, somewhere to call home.

There were several candidates for a home for the Club, but a move westwards to the Cotswolds became reality when the Prescott estate, originally owned by the Earl of Ellenborough, passed from its then current owners (the Royd family) to the overview of Tom Rolt – better known as L.T. C. Rolt, the author and competitive driver. Rolt persuaded several backers, notably the recently formed Vintage Sports-Car Club (VS-CC), to consider relocating events to the Prescott estate and its natural amphitheatre of a site, after it had initially passed to an interim owner after the Royds had sold up. Tom Rolt was a joint founder of the VS-CC and pivotal in the BOC. Despite being a car fanatic and a sporting car man at that, Rolt was concerned about the environment and took great interest in the countryside –

Two 1926 Bugattis show off the essential Ettore design language.

hardly a surprise then that he should fall in love with Prescott's Cotswold setting amid a landscape of domed hills, gentle valleys and views of the distant Malverns.

Rolt drove GN, Alvis, and Bugatti cars with great verve. But the VS-CC was in its own infancy at this time and side-stepped the opportunity to purchase Prescott. But part of the deal to secure Prescott for the Club was in giving the VS-CC the rights to run one completely independent event a year.

Significantly, it was the long driveway up to the main Prescott residence that was the lure – an ideal 'hill climb' suitable for resurfacing and of far more importance than the house at the top of it. Mr Cecil 'Sam' Clutton was to become pivotal in the process that led to the Bugatti Owners Club occupying the Prescott site; the Giles brothers would in late 1936 become the vital benefactors of the BOC by providing the money to secure the estate, its drive, and then renting the site to the Club at a low annual rent. Clutton would go on to prove the point about Prescott being about people because not only would he compete in the first true Prescott hill climb event in 1938 (on the original 880 yards course), he would, fifty years later, drive the same car – a 12 Litre 1908 Itala – on the 'long' 1,227 yards course at Prescott's 50th anniversary meeting in May 1988!

2018 saw the Club celebrate its 80th anniversary – and a worldwide membership of over 2,000 Bugatti owners, enthusiasts and utterly addicted fanatics.

After some work on the track and its surface, by the spring of 1938, Prescott had become a true home to the Club, and also to the annual VS-CC main event. So began the true 'magic' of Prescott – only temporarily halted by the Second World War. The very first meeting at Prescott on 10 April 1938 was a 'closed' affair for BOC members only and was an informal opening party. Of note, the April Spring Rally at Prescott started at Cheltenham where 130 members and guests lunched at the Queens Hotel. They then drove in convoy to Prescott, led by Colonel Godfrey Giles in his Type 18 Bugatti 'Black Bess', to have a look at their new home and try some informal timed runs. Ian Craig was to prove fastest in his 5-litre 'Bachelier' Bugatti in 55.58 seconds.

The 'names'

George Abecassis, Arthur Baron, Kenneth Bear, Roy Blomfield, Jack Lemon Burton, H.G. Conway, Neil Corner, Ian Craig, Joe Fry, Peter Hampton, Mike Hatton, Ninian Hyslop, Elizabeth Junek, Hugh Conway, Kaye Don, Barrie Price, Eddie Greenall (Lord Daresbury), John Marks, Mike Oliver, Tony Rippon, A. F. River Fletcher, Bob Roberts, The Hon F.J. Somerset (Lord Raglan), Geoffrey St John, Peter Stubberfield, Ronnie Symondson, Teddy Milvain, Ken Wharton, Frank Wall, Gordon Lind Walker, A. C. Whincop – these were just some of the names that helped carve the Bugatti niche upon Prescott's tarmac (and sometimes its turf!) across the decades.

Prior to this era, A.F. River Fletcher had done much to promote the marque and Prescott itself. He drove a Type 35B (non-supercharged), a Type 59 and campaigned an ERA. Peter Stubberfield was a legend up Prescott hill – in 1951, he beat Jean-Pierre Wimille's Bugatti 'works' car's pre-war time, and in 1957 set not just the fastest time of the day (FTD), but a record that would not be broken for nearly twenty-five years.

Back in August 1938, both Jean Bugatti and Jean Pierre Wimille were booked in at the Queens Hotel, Cheltenham, prior to arriving at Prescott in a whirl of blue paint and blue overalls. After heavy rain, just before 2 pm the Clerk of the Course drove Earl Howe, the RAC Steward, up the Prescott hill in Colonel Giles' recently acquired Type 57S (GU 7). The crowd was rewarded with an afternoon of exciting climbs with further course records culminating with Raymond Mays in Class 7 achieving 46.16 seconds!

Finally, with Class 8, the bigger cars came up to the Start line. The 'works' Bugatti Type 50 built under the 1937 G.P. formula but with a supercharger fitted, was brought up to the line, an electrical starter was inserted in the offside just forward of the cockpit and its magnetos, and she fired up in a blast of Bugatti sound.

A consultation then took place and Jean Bugatti, with a blast of sound, he was away. His first climb in 47.50 seconds was significant considering how unsuitable the big, long wheelbase car really was for Prescott: on his second run he got down to 46.69, a matter of .55 seconds slower than Raymond Mays. Wimille was disappointed that he had not done better, but Jean Bugatti was philosophical:

'I am sorry,' he said, 'I have brought a car that is unsuitable for your hill. Next year we will bring over a 1 ½ litre car – one of our new ones – and I hope that we shall do better.'

In the war that ensued within a year, Wimille served in the French Air Force until the fall of France, then in the French Resistance and finally in North Africa. The driving career of this great driver came to an end when he was killed in an accident during practice for the 1949 Buenos Aires Grand Prix. His life and achievements are celebrated at Michel Pont's wonderful museum at the Chateau de Savigny-les-Beaune in eastern France (take exit 24 off the main Autoroute 24).

The magnificence of the Wimille Bugatti at Prescott can be seen in the photographs herein.

A typical Prescott story is that of Ronnie Symondson who bought his first Bugatti (a Brescia Modifeé) in 1925, drove his ex-Andre Embiricos Bugatti Type 57S at Prescott's first-ever meeting on 15 May 1938 and drove the same car at Prescott in his final competitive event on 4 September 1983. In fact, Symondson was given competitor number 1 at the first Prescott meet on 15 May 1938 and went on to compete in 112 Prescott meetings. He was Club chairman for six years in the 1960s and a definite 'fixture' of Prescott. Ronnie also owned an elegant Vanvooren-bodied Type 57S drop-head that he also punted up Prescott's hill.

Like so many of the names herein, Symondson's association with the BOC and presence at Prescott would span five decades from the 1930s to the 1980s. Similarly, Peter Hampton's vital BOC contribution spanned from 1934 to 1991.

The Milvain family were also Prescott regulars in its first era and in recent years Tim Milvain has kept the family name on the Prescott tarmac. Such is the dedication and addiction of Prescott and Bugatti.

Amid the Bugattis, we must not forget the presence at Prescott of the ERA cars. On yet another sunny day, Prescott's 50th birthday in 1988 saw

From the Captain's seat: grab a magneto and go.

W. 'Bill' Morris break the course record in the unlimited class with a time of 51.8 seconds in his B Type ERA. Today the ERA line-up at Prescott causes many hairs to rise at their spectacular sight. And excitement also rises when the delightful Amilcars trundle about too, notably Ian Patton's UC 53. But then the serenity is shattered by a pre-war Bugatti, or a new Chiron; only to be further punctured by the 500cc 'Specials' – or a 1920s JAP-engined insect chain-sawing its way up the hill in a blur of hill climb memorabilia. Recently, the giant 'Beast of Turin' FIAT driven by Duncan Pittway has deafened a few sparrows.

Bugaires

Back in Prescott's post-war partying heydays, what of the wonderfully named 'Bugaires'? This was a team of three men, Bugatti owners who campaigned across the national hill climb schedule and made Prescott their home. Peter Gaskell, Mike Hatton and David Vickers-Jones were the Bugaires trio who made 1950s forays up Prescott Hill, notably in number '125' – the eight-cylinder Type 35 with an extravagant side exhaust manifold. They also ran a Type 37 (UA 7310).

Hardly elitist, the men based themselves out of the White Swan pub in Harbourne near Birmingham. Bugaires team photographer and general factotum was a man named Griff Bury. The team made its last runs in 1957

A series of boat tails and details rest in afternoon light in the Paddock.

and then split up – with two drivers (Gaskell and Hatton) transferring to the Cooper single-seater class with notable success.

If you thought Bugatti owners were all 'posh', try remembering Jim Berry from that hotbed of elitism, Rochdale! Jim ran a Type 55 (AUL 23) for a decade from the mid-Fifties into the 'Sixties. Jim made a time of 46.7 at Prescott – which no one would look down their nose at...

All these men (and the occasional women) were sent off on their ways from Prescott in its post-war high by a team of helpers, Club officials, marshals, and the starter. Russell Ashby was the well-known starter, and the Hartley-Smith duo of father Jack and son George were Prescott's start line duo of renown for many years. Jack was official RAC timekeeper and event Steward. More recently, Prescott's Bugatti action has been supplied by a legion of names, and many of them can be seen in action across these pages. Some of them have been coming to Prescott for so long they are, dare it be said, of a certain age.

Veteran Bugatti believer Barrie Price cannot go unmentioned for his exploits!

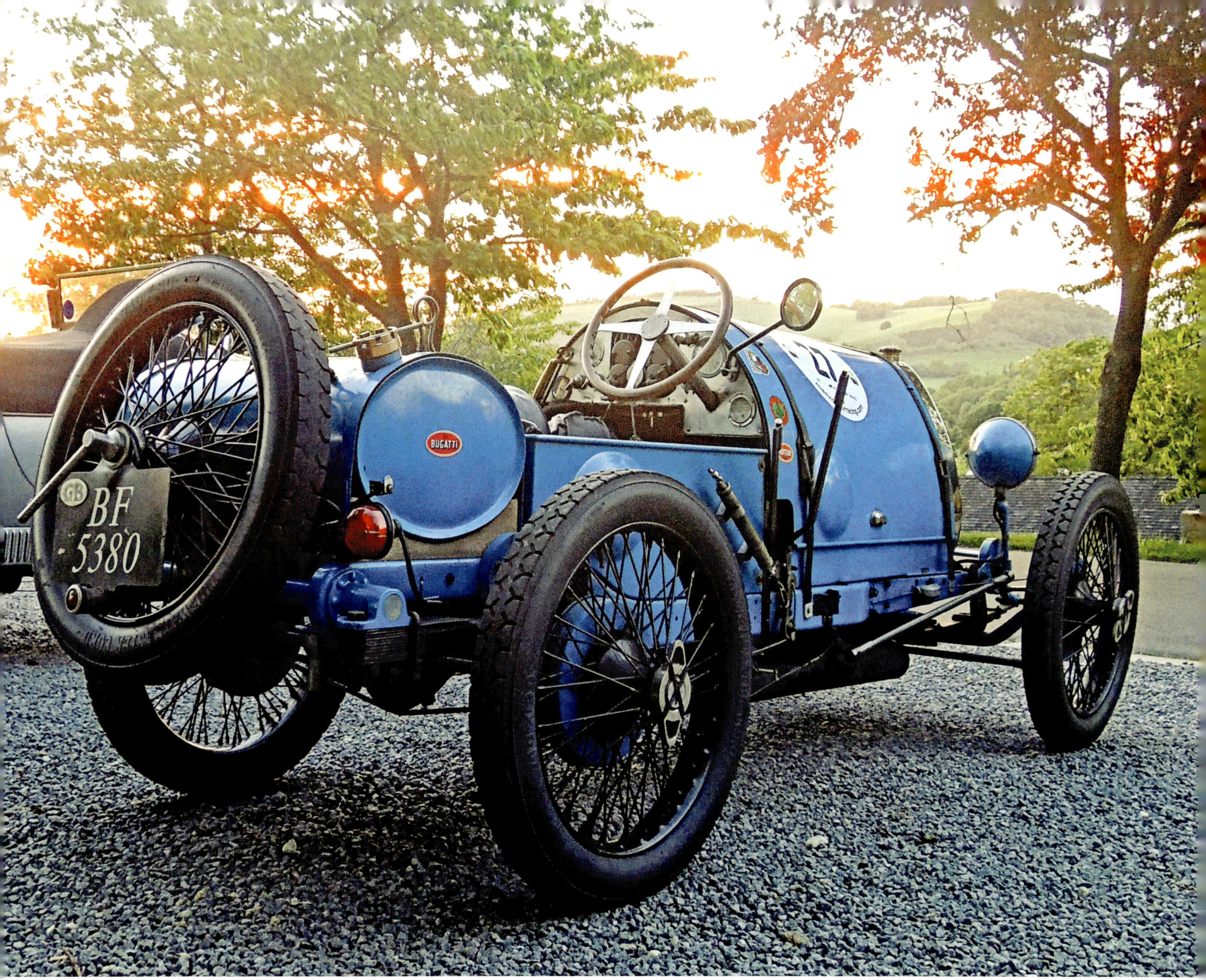

Prescott's parking terrace is bathed in evening light as a Bugatti slumbers.

The ultimate Bugatti bollide? The rare twin-cam supercharged Type 50B ready to pounce in blue. J-P Wimille drove one at Prescott in the heady days of pre-war hill climbing. Bugatti made several such cars, each with specification developments.

MLP 802, Derek Hitchman's Type 37 of noted heritage, rests in pure style on the Prescott terrace.

Mike and Jakub captured cornering Bugatti style – hang on tight.

Two more pilots in earnest as the Bugatti crouches and powers away.

Going into Ettore's as long shadows cast, slow in fast out.

Charles Trevelyan 'the Club's Chairman' owns this Type 37 Chassis 37282, seen as it scythes into Prescott for another great day out.

Julian Eckersley at the wheel of a blue Bugatti.

Edmund Burgess on the Paddock grid in his Type 51 – on four wheels.

A quiet afternoon as the sun lowers itself over a contemplative Prescott. Roland Duce's Type 57S rests beyond the racers. A typical scene from another brilliant blue day under sunny skies.

Mike Marshall gets ready as the right crowd prove there is no crowding – just Bugatti adulation.

All the action – the Prescott 'atmosphere' at its best as three types of Bugatti jostle.

Concentrate: the brakes might be tardy!

Julian Eckersley tends his Bug! More oil needed Julian?

Gillian Howard-Orchard with Derek, going up the hill at Prescott in times past. Gilly has been pivotal in the formation of the 'Friends of Prescott' as a fund-raising body.

Power out of the Esses; pure Bugatti magic for BF 5898.

Julia de Baldanza – Bugatti racer and a woman with a Bugatti passion – arrives at Prescott in the 'Lidia' car, chassis 40623. Built by Jean Bugatti for his sister Lidia, this is a unique Type 40 coupé fitted with a supercharger from a Type 37A. Called a 'Fiacre' style, it reflects early horse-drawn carriage styling themes as transposed by Ettore.

A Type 40 A chassis with drophead body style chassis 40929 was last cited in the Bugatti Register to an R.J. De Little who acquired the car in 1989.

The patina of Bugatti, the Type 13 campaigned by Peter Livesey across recent Prescott years, still looks utterly pure.

Janet Missen, and the family's Bugattis, leave Prescott after another day at the crucible of British Bugatti addiction. Janet and her blue Bugatti T30 are essential elements in the enthusiasm of Bugatti.

The essence of Bugatti.

Tim Dutton of Ivan Dutton Ltd awaits take off in the 1933 Type 54 4.9 Litre at Prescott.

Jean Bugatti chats to Earl Howe. Behind, Jean Pierre Wimille talks to a mechanic as the big Type 50 Bugatti awaits another turn up the hill. (Photo: BOC)

Above: It is 1947 and this elegant lady in her Bugatti Type 35 is a member of the Milvain family. (Photo: BOC/Dacre Stibbs)

Above right: A faded rare shot of the Scuderia Lemon Burton in action; Jack Lemon Burton's green car seen in the May 1939 meeting. (Photo: BOC)

Right: Jim Berry goes through the Esses in a T55 . (Photo: BOC/Eggleston)

Tony Vickers-Jones, one of the 'Bugaires', at Prescott on 5 May 1955. (Photo: BOC)

1953 at the 9th International meeting at Prescott and the Symondson car heads the Howarth car GNE 801 in the cavalcade. GNE 801 was later sold to provide start-up funds for the Bugatti Trust. (Photo: BOC)

This very rare photograph shows the 'geodetic' type, glazed coupé hard top that Eric Giles is said to have created for their Corsica bodied car, with due regard to aerodynamics and visibility. Colonel Giles and his brother Eric must have made an impact upon arrival in this! (Photo: BOC)

A gaggle of essential Bugattis in the Paddock, seen in its timeless mode – at the Bugatti Owners' Club at Prescott's 80th Anniversary celebrations.

Leaning into the turn as another Brescia shows off the ovoid tumblehome body shape as Bugattis scatter.

A Type 59 displays its clever wire wheel combination design in this detailed study. The spokes only carried a wheel load in one axis – radial, whereas the torque loads were held by teeth placed between the rim and the backing plate. A brilliant torque/twist solution that eschewed cast alloy spokes of 'normal' Bugatti preference.

Janet Missen and her car on the Prescott lawn. The dedicated Bugatti owner studies a working straight eight that needed a small adjustment before its 100 mile drive home. Almost a daily driver then! Janet's daughter also turns up in her Bugatti.

The Hon. Sir Michael Kadoorie scythes away from Prescott in his wonderful two-tone blue T57C after attending the 80th event. The straight-eight sounded wonderful as take-off speed spooled up.

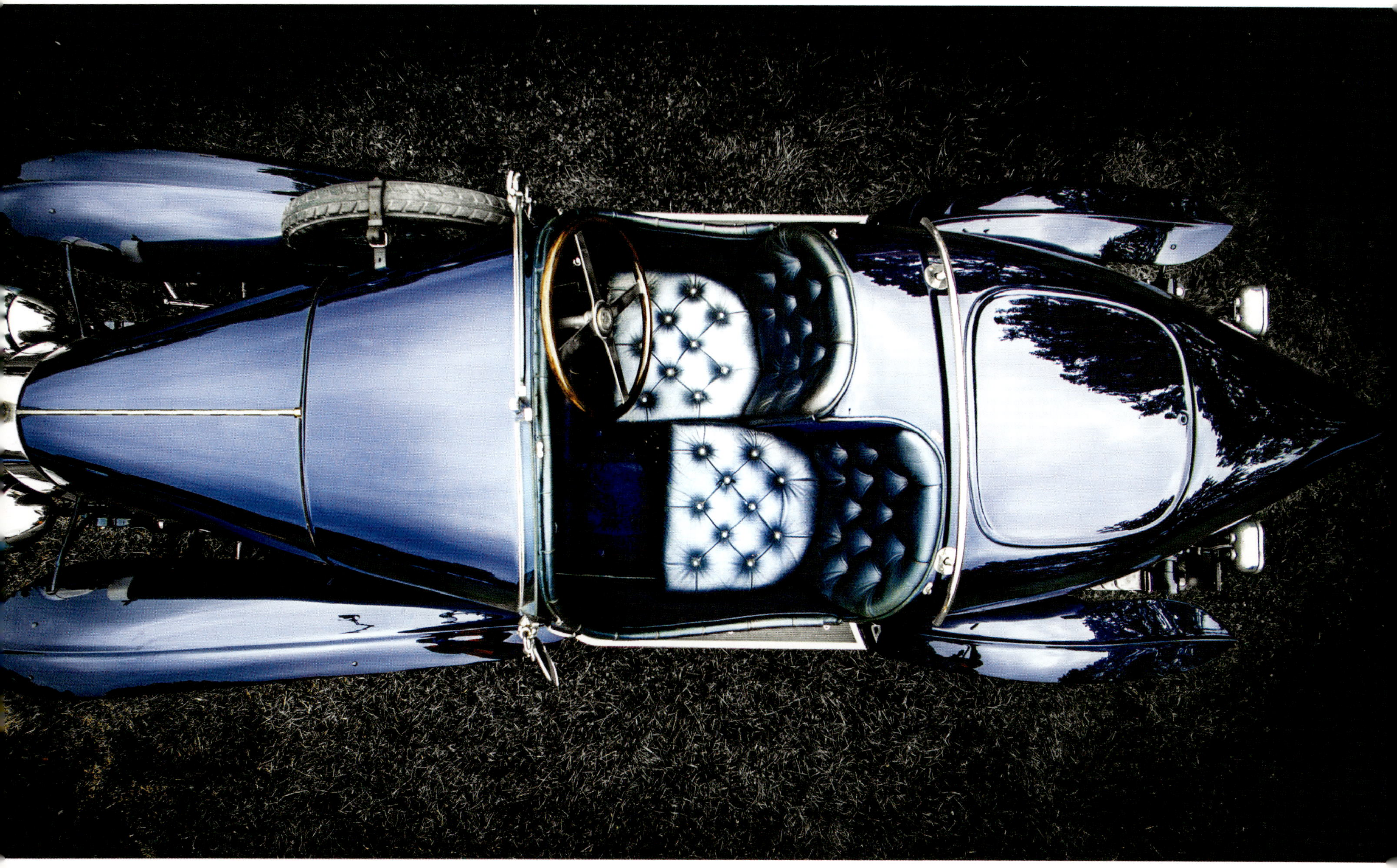

Overhead view of buttoned leather and staggered seating, Bugatti blue in sport style.

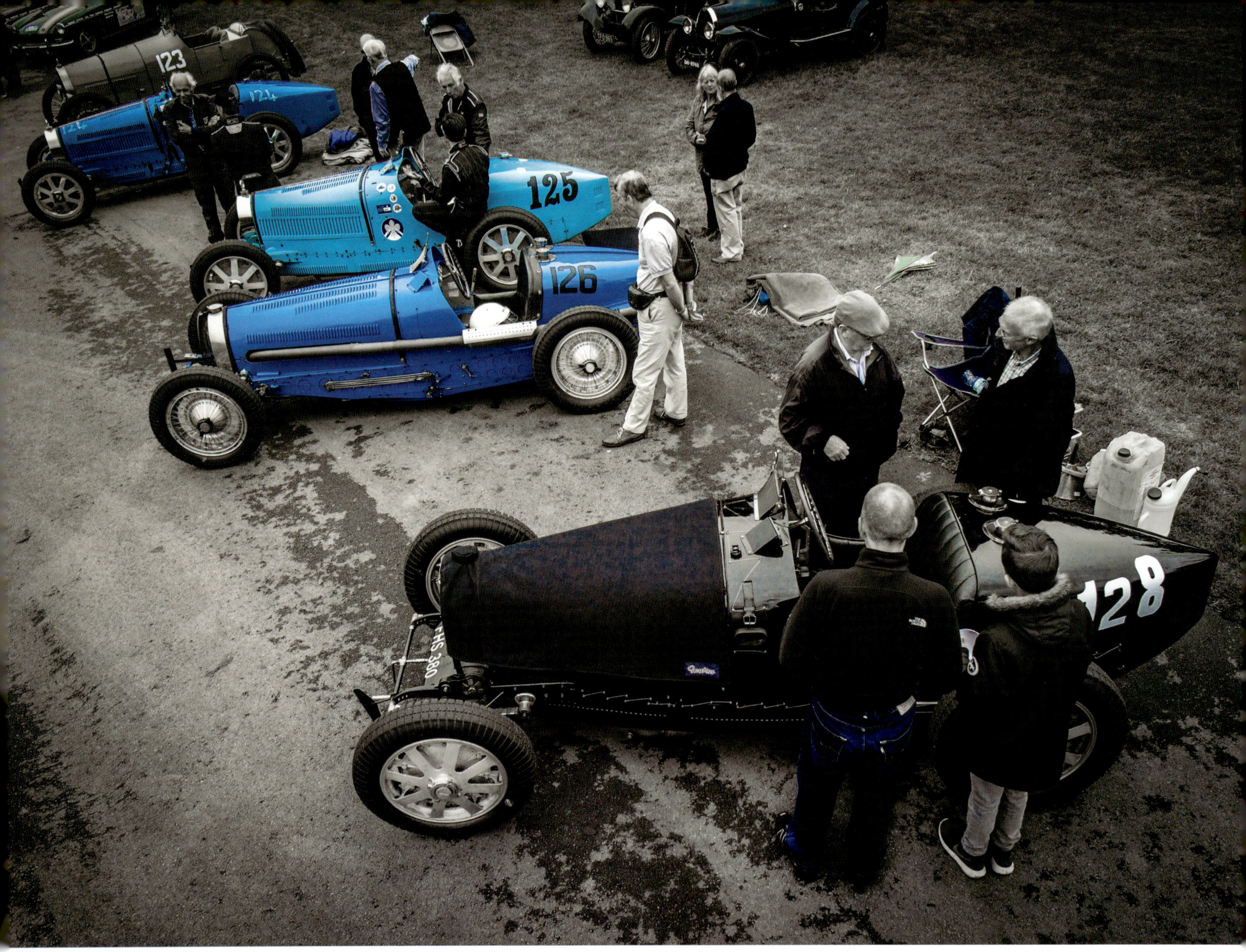

Blue in the paddock sees Messrs Marshall, Huntley, Gentry, et al await squadron scramble.

A Sport Tourer T40-series turns into Prescott as it arrives for the BOC summer gathering. The tiled barn behind is probably older than the car.

Keith Knight and family with their Type 49 3.3litre are Prescott supporters par excellence . They often bring a Citroen SM too!

Dashboard delight: pure Bugatti design.

John Huntley in his 1925 Type 30 sits beside the Jarvis-bodied Type 40 as they head up a Bugatti line up. Pure Prescott magic.

Eyes right, ahem! Prescott atmosphere.

Julian Eckersley and the blue T13 Brescia a popular fitting in the Paddock.

Above and opposite: The Brescia races up the hill and out of the Esses.

286

T13'bolster' tank detail – pure Bugatti design genius.

The Bugatti varietals rest on the parking terrace awaiting the next climb.

Above and overleaf: The long course with long shadows as the Brescia goes in and out of Ettore's.

150
BS 9778

Talking of blue Brescia brilliance.

Short wheelbase, blue, nimble and essential Bugatti design.

A novel oiler!

Getting ready to go – from the cockpit.

175
BUGATTI

Above and previous page: Mike Ward and the 1921 1,500cc Type 13 prepare for the next run. Open a Bugatti panel and men will gather.

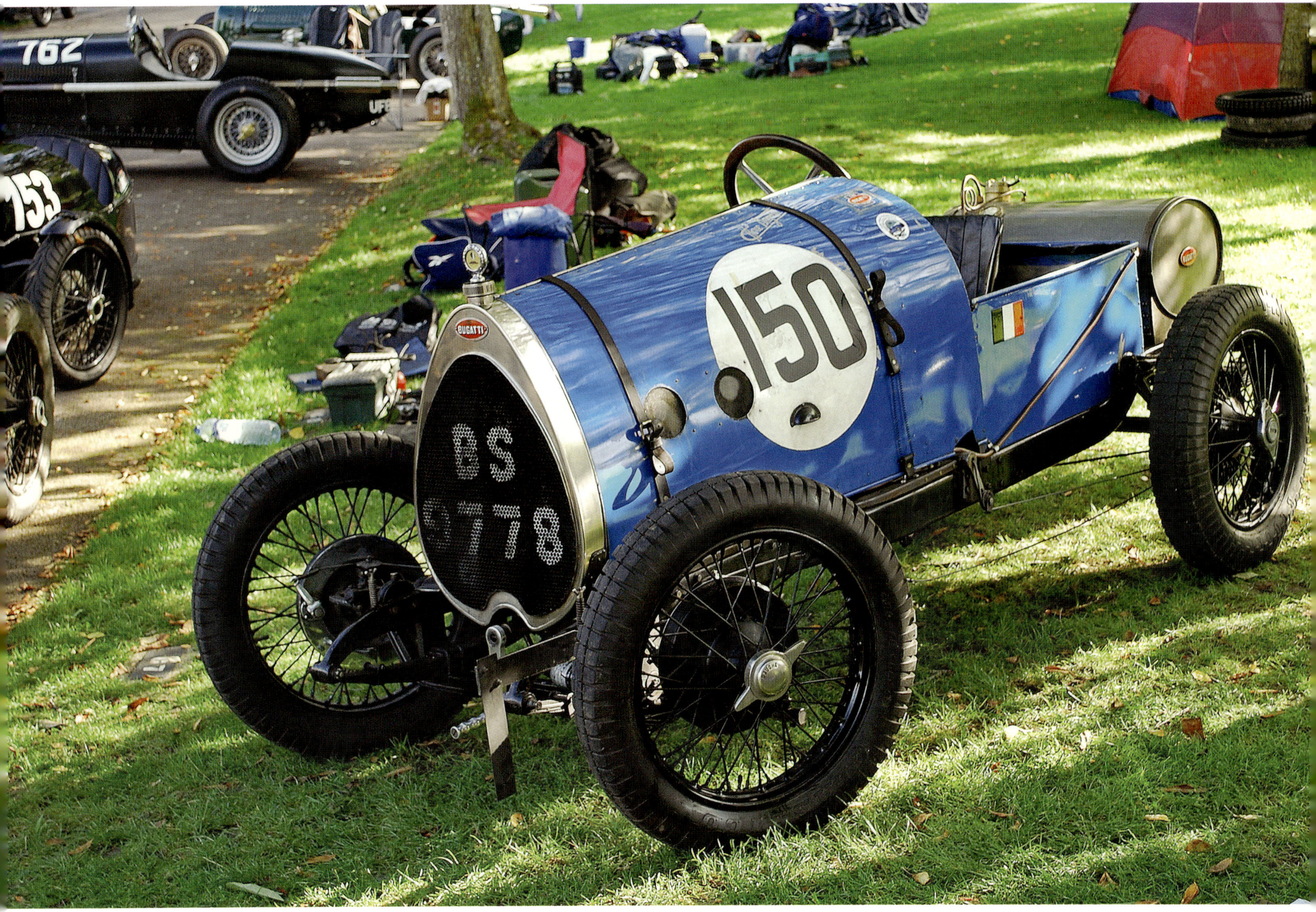

Pure Bugattism amid afternoon shadows and a quintessential Prescott Paddock scene.

Above, opposite and overleaf: Adam Ward's 1926 Type 40 has a long Spanish provenance based in Madrid – hence the pre-war symbol painted on the grille. The design of the body may be of factory or French carrosserie origin.

119
M-24851
GB

27
25

M-24851
GB
SV 9038

Adam fettles the Spanish Bugatti.

This Spanish symbol has long been in evidence on the car's front grille. The symbol may relate to allegiances in Madrid in the 1930s era…

Above, left and overleaf: Dashboard delights: This series of moments captures the brilliance of Bugatti dashboard or 'tableau d' board' design motifs and the exquisite instrumentation.

HUILE
BUGATTI
MANOMETRE G.F. Bte S.G.D.G.
KILOMETRES

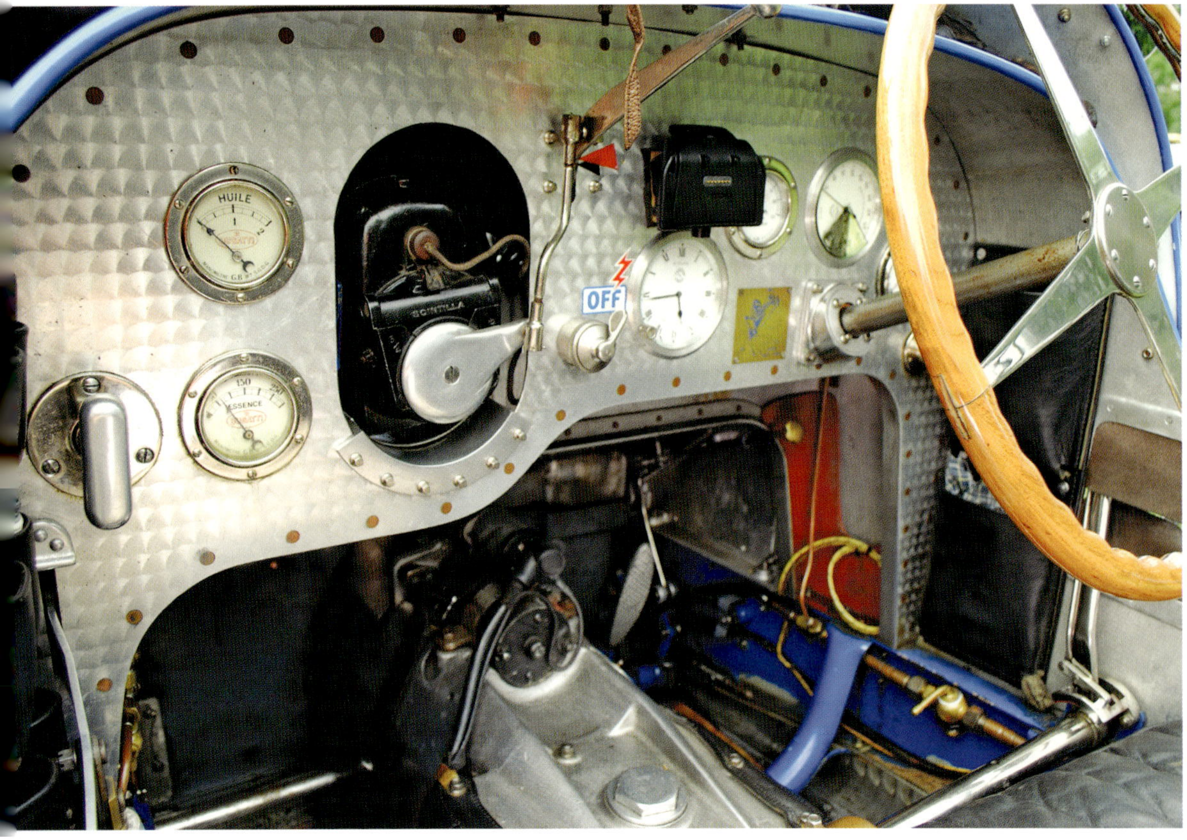
HUILE
ESSENCE
OFF

TOURS
x 100
FABRIQUÉ EN SUISSE
IGN. FREE OFF

Above and overleaf: Mike Marshall from Gloucester always adds to the interest and camaraderie at Prescott in his 1927 Type 35B.

PRIZE DRAW RAFFLE
DRIVER:
MIKE MARSHALL
CPW
940
FHS 380

CHAPTER 2

Old & New

In recent times, new names and old cars with new owners have been drawn inexorably to Prescott. Some have been coming so long, they can claim their pension, but then some of their cars are approaching their 80th, 90th, or even 100th birthdays. There is only one thing older than an ageing Bugattiste – and that is a Bugatti itself! But the VS-CC membership might top the ton...

The original 1938 short course remains as it should (but with a newer surface), the post-1960 long course with its new loop and Ettore's corner at the end of the Orchard valley field, and the less familiar cross-over course also supply differing fun and differing times.

The 1970s-1980s also saw H.R.G. – Hugh R.G. Conway, the son of H.G. Conway – drive a Type 37B (YN 5834) on a regular basis at Prescott. Conway senior, a BOC member since 1952, had, with Barrie Price, founded the Bugatti Trust and written numerous books about Bugatti.

Bernard Kain competed at Prescott in Bugattis in his Type 35 across the years from 1959 to the 1980s. Like so many other men mentioned here, he just kept on coming back in a Bugatti and replaced the late Alan Howarth on the Bugatti Trust's founding team. Bob Roberts was one of the four people who formed the original committee for the founding and advancement of the Bugatti Trust in the late 1980s. Alan Howarth was one of the others in that gang of four. He latterly sold the Type 35 C known as the 'Genie' from its registration of 'GNE' to help fund the start of the Bugatti Trust. Jack Lemon Burton, once of 'Scuderia Lemon Burton', was by the 1980s still driving at Prescott and president of the BOC. Geoffrey St John would become an authority on Bugatti and be a technical advisor to the Bugatti Trust. The bronze of Ettore Bugatti that resides at the Bugatti Trust was paid for by Frank Wall's family in memory of Frank's many happy years at Prescott in his Type 35B.

A. Rippon, G. St John, I. Preston, B. Price, J. Marks, Sir J. Venables-Llewelyn, H. Conway and A.C. Trevelyan are the key names of the Club's late twentieth century tenure and function – and into the new millennium. A Council exists beneath the offices of President, President Emeritus, and Chair. So a team of guardians ensure the future is as rewarding as the past.

Although a modest man who would hate to be spotlighted, one of the regular pilots at Prescott is Mike Preston – who can be seen driving Bugattis in the photos that accompany this narrative. Mike has been around Bugattis for years and is based at nearby Cheltenham. His father, Ian, owned an ex-Stubberfield Type 50 with drop-head Nef bodywork, latterly rebuilt to original style; the car had raced at Le Mans in 1935 and then passed through several BOC members' ownership (including Kenneth Bear and Stafford East) until Ian Preston acquired it. At the BOC's meeting in 1972, Ian drove the Type 50 as a preface to a decade driving the Type 35B at

Sir John speeds in. Another classic arrives – the car and the driver!

Prescott. Mike spent many of his younger years under his father's Bugattis and drove the Type 50 at the BOC's 75th anniversary meeting in June 2004. In 2006, this car won its class at the Le Mans Classic and was driven all the way home from France without any issues.

'I've been crawling around these things for years, since childhood,' says Mike. 'I think I was eight when I first started helping with the Type 50. Our car was often worked on late into the night – beyond midnight before a Prescott event. I often crawled into all the tight places and when it started up and all those mechanical bits I had put in started to fly around I would take a step back in case the split pin I had put in came out!'

Today, Mike Preston is a Bugatti owner/driver who willingly gives up his time to talk to all-comers as they wander over and stare at the Type 35B as he preps the car prior for a Prescott drive.

Another 'Mike' is Michael Marshall from Gloucester – he too is a long-established Bugatti man who gives his time to strangers who are transfixed by his 1927 Type 35B. 'Mike powers around Pardon' seems to be an eternal caption.

Stephen Gentry in the Bo Williams T35B leans into the Esses.

Mike Ward is a regular in his 1,500cc 1921 Type 13. John Huntley from Bicester is another Prescott fixture with his 1925, 1,991cc Type 30 – the grey Bugatti – eschewing as it does traditional bright blue. Adam Ward is a Prescott regular accompanied by his rare 1926 Type 40 that has a Spanish pre-war to post-war ownership history and an unusual body that must be of factory (or French *carrosserie*) origin. Back in the 1990s, the Type 13 (NX 6600) of David Sewell was a regular sight at Prescott. Sewell was the second curator of the Bugatti Trust after its first curator, Rosemary Burke, retired from the role. Sewell had worked in collaboration with Conway and had produced the second edition of the Bugatti Register in 1989 and went on to assist Jonathan Wood with his Cugnot-award-winning book, *Bugatti The Man and his Marque*.

Tim Dutton runs several Bugattis and a world-renowned Bugatti sales and restoration emporium – Ivan Dutton Ltd. Ivan was another Prescott fixture in years past – his son Tim is the same thing today. Of interest, Ivan created 'Bilko' – a Type 44 rebuilt mostly from original parts as a special. Ivan competed in the 1980s and in September 1985 set a new Bugatti record for the Prescott long course at 53.20 seconds in a Type 51 owned by David Heimann. Ivan also did 52.86 seconds in a Type 35 in June 1997.

Julian Majzub (of Blockley Tyres fame) is an Allard fancier and a Bugatti-owning fan and, in 1991 and 1998, set Bugatti, Prescott short course records of 43. 06 seconds and 42.91 seconds respectively, in his Type 35B.

Blue amid the Bugattistes

Above: Rupert Marks and passenger sans headgear as the Type 59 gets long and low in late light – a true, blue streak.

Below: Coming round Pardon with the crowds looking across the fields. Pure Sang Prescott.

He continues to hare up the hill to date. The current outright record for a Bugatti at Prescott on the long course is 51.97 seconds set by Charles Dean in a Type 51 (2,300cc) on 27 June 1994, but wonderful as the Type 25, 37, or 50s-series are, we can also find true delight in the early, smaller Bugattis – notably the Brescia Types.

Janet Missen has more than one Bugatti in the family and is a regular at Prescott amid a Bugatti enthusiasm which saw her formerly write *Bugantics* – no easy task and one subsequently taken up by John Staveley. Prescott, its people, and the VS-CC all miss the vibrant contributions to so many aspects of the story by the late Sue Staveley. VS-CC Head of the ladies Marshals start line team, Chief Assembly Marshal – as paddock 'boss' (herding cats they call it!), Jaguar Drivers Club contributor, problem solver, and all round positive influence, Sue's contribution via the VS-CC's events (that began in the early 1980s) remains an essential part of the Prescott story.

Other recent 'names' of Prescott Bugatti exploits include: Alex Ames, John Boulton, Colin Bullock, William Clarke, Neil Corner, John Day, Tom Dewhurst, George Dewhurst, Simon Diffey and Sarah Adams Diffey, Desmond Dillon, Derek Hitchman, Derek Howard-Orchard, Mark Miller, Locky McKenzie, Bruce Stops, Paul Tebbett. All hare up the hill in Bugattis of various hues and types.

Mike Preston gives a young lad the Bugatti ride he won in a Prescott prize draw. Hopefully it will inspire a lifetime's Bugatti enthusiasm.

4.9 Litres and supercharged. Very rare and very special.

Roger Thomas and his family own a very nice Type 37A which always appears on their Bugatti spare parts, bits-and-bobs stand in the Orchard at Prescott. Roger, a BOC man, is also an early1930s era MG enthusiast – the cars not the man! The Thomas family's Bugatti spare parts and memorabilia stand is a true vintage fixture at Prescott and always worth a look – but bring money!

Driving the hill

'Keep it clean, go smooth' – such has been the eternal advice for making rapid progress up Prescott. Sheer power and brute force can make a car fast, but if the driver is constantly jiggling the controls and making on-off power, brake, gear, and steering applications, then progress is unstable, ragged and time-consuming.

'Prescott's bends are deceptive,' says a veteran of the hill. 'You need to brake at just the right time – not too early and not too late, otherwise you will upset the car for that bend and fail to get it set up for the next. This is very true out of Orchard into Ettore's or Pardon. It's a bit like guiding a thoroughbred horse around a show jumping ring – you need to perfect every foot of your progress prior to making it. And just when you think you have got it right, one mistake can have the tail skidding or the nose ploughing on and the car heading for the foliage, this is particularly so through Orchard, into and out of Pardon and the Esses.' So says our expert, who wishes to remain anonymous.

Peter Stubberfield, for so long the course record holder, also said that smooth progress was the way to make the fastest time at Prescott. Braking too soon or too late was, thought Stubberfield, likely to impede speed.

The 3,257cc Type 59 Grand Prix was leaner and meaner, and had an added 'spine'. Oh, and it did 155mph/250km/h. Six were constructed for racing and a few 'specials'. Earl Howe owned a T59. This is the Marks family car and is based upon an original chassis.

Getting your gear changes and throttle settings correct – or not – can make or break a time by hundredths of a second, say the experts on the hill. Even the Start straight can catch the unwary. Sydney Allard got off too fast and, after a bit of a wobble under acceleration, slammed into the footbridge legs on the seemingly innocuous straight. He also once overcooked it up beyond the Esses and rolled over the edge and took a tumble down the hill. Allard was again lucky to survive. Edmund Burgess had a spectacular crash in his Type 13 out of Pardon and half-rolled the car up against the banking with his head and shoulders seemingly taking the brunt of the impact. Edmund commented that having survived, he was off for a pint! As you would...

Pardon is a low speed bend yet requires a forensic entry and exit technique.

We should not forget that it was at Prescott that Sir Stirling Moss got his first proper competitive driving experiences in 1949 – his initial blooding into hill climbing. He was tutored on the arts of mastering Prescott by Sydney Allard – who would become that year's British Hill Climb Champion – and placed at Le Mans soon afterwards. Maybe Stirling's smooth style was nurtured here – with a bit of Allard tutoring?

In 2017, Prescott again held the 'Rob Roy' event. This bi-annual meeting was the idea (in 2007) of two BOC members, John Passmore and Joy Rainey, and is a shared, twinning affair between Australia's Rob Roy hill climb circuit near Melbourne, Victoria State, and Prescott. The Rob Roy course is in fact one year older than Prescott (from 1937) and a similar length. Shared hill climbing competition are common to both.

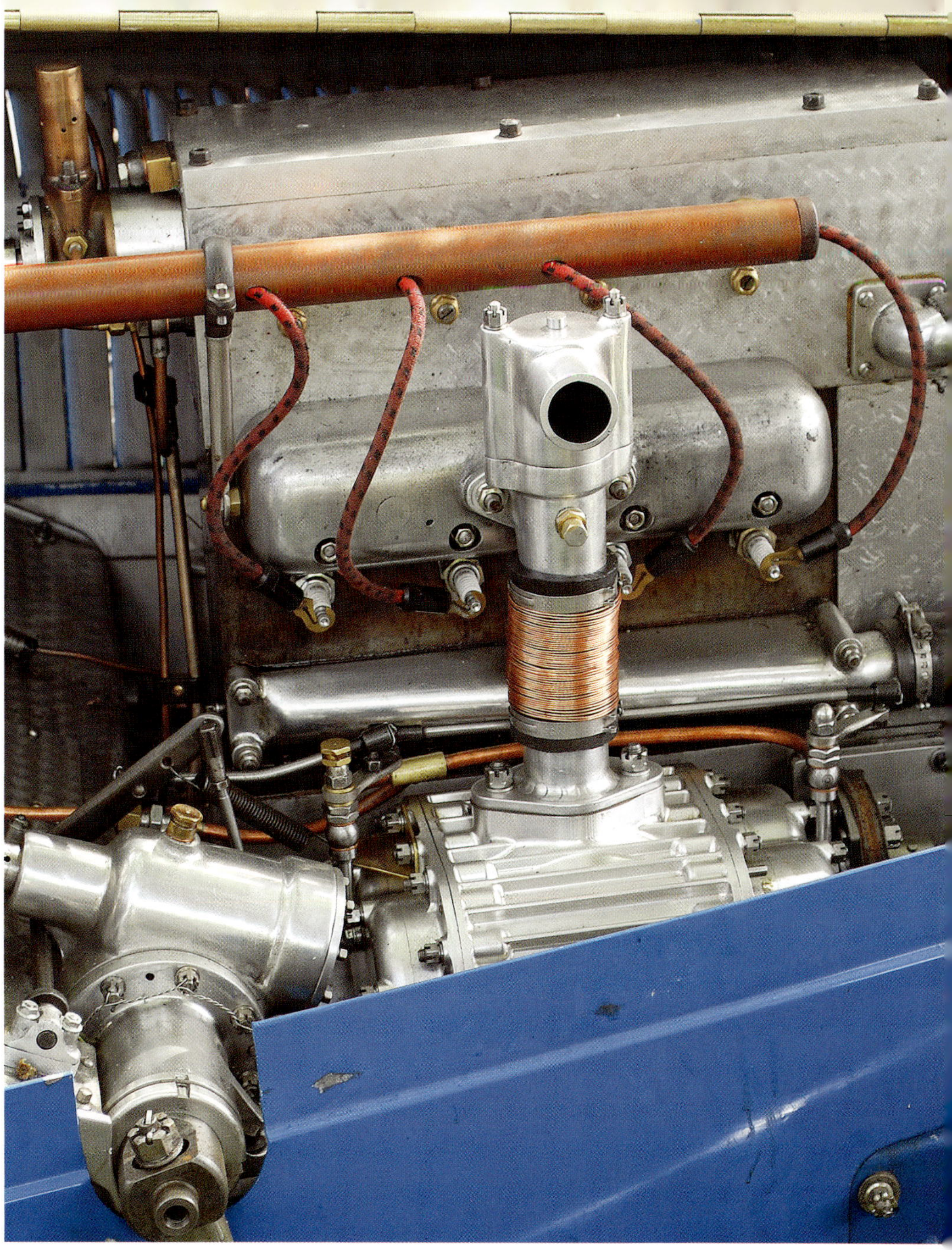

Short-block delight: how to keep your Bugatti engine as it was intended. This one is in the Type 37A owned by Roger Thomas. Pure perfection of the Bugatti 'elegance of function' – to coin a phrase once coined by a certain German car maker...

SY6 in all its glory on a hot summer day at Prescott. Polished alloy, shimmering steel, blue paint, and Bugatti design. Improvement would be superfluous and unlikely. According to its current owner, one previous (wartime) owner sold the car to finance the purchase of a wedding ring. Let's hope it was worth it!

John Horton's delightful Type 38 goes up the hill out of Pardon with proof of the Bugatti affection across the generations.

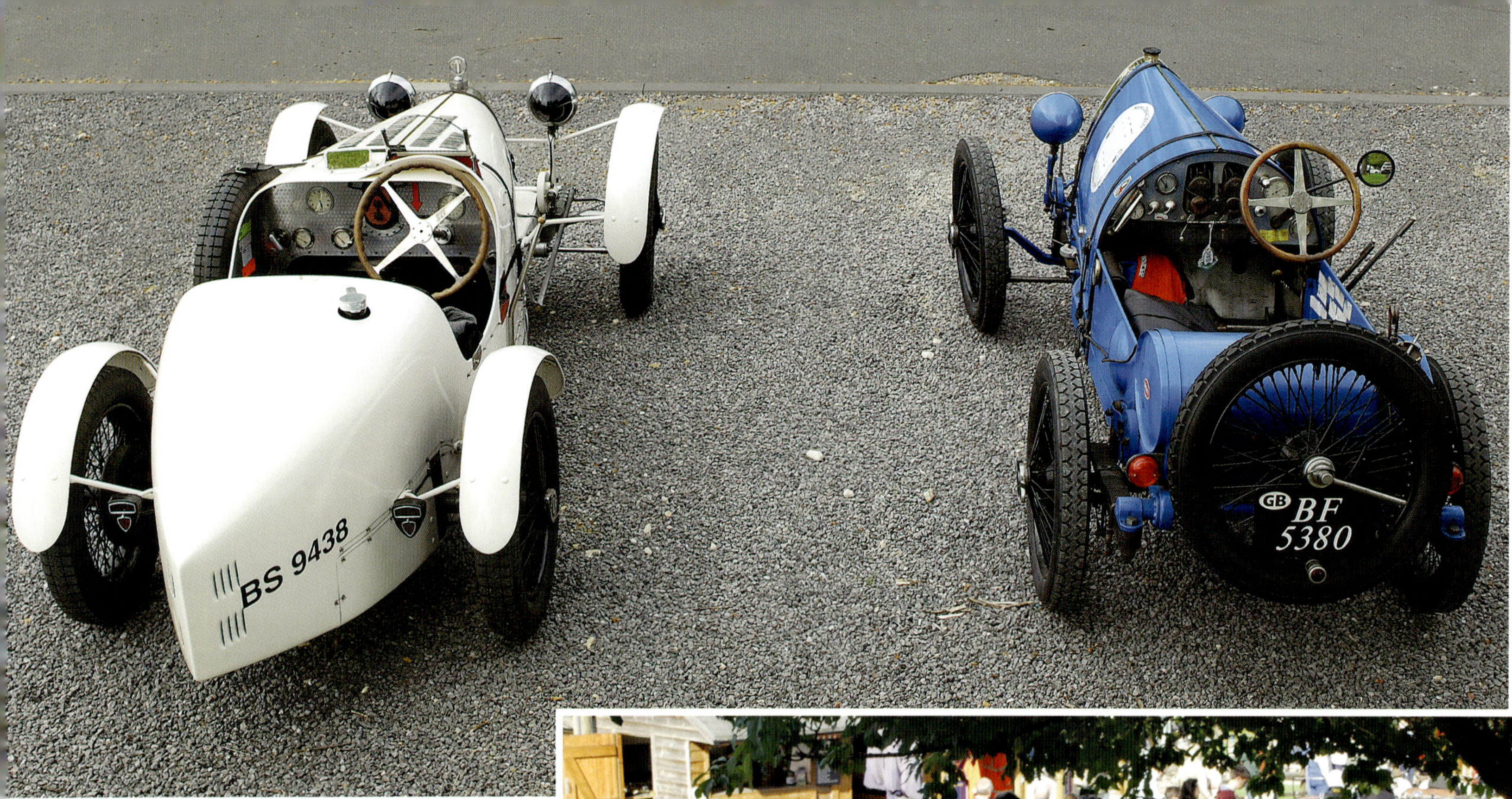

Above and right: White Bugattis are rather rare and this one has a female pilot.

Tim Dutton in the Type 54 seen from a new angle.

Tim Dutton and his passenger's faces seem to be under the effect of G-force as the 4.9 litre supercharged charges away from the Start. Proper power!

Prepare for take-off!

Leaving Prescott, Mike Preston in DAR 349, the 1931 short-chassis, sports T50 (chassis number 50143) – a car that ran at Le Mans in 1935. Mike has also a T35B and the ex-G.St John T43.

Mike Marshall really gets the T35B going out of Pardon in the heat. Hang on tight!

Prescott, almost empty, the Clubhouse behind with few lingering members.

Dashboard delight: Peter Mullin's immaculate California registered T54 turned up at the 80th Anniversary event, but stayed under cover.

An unusual view of the Paddock as Bugatti blue rests.

Type 57S (Gangloff body) interior. Simple but efficient.

So finely tuned, chassis and suspension details display Ettore's forensic design ideas applied as production reality.

Coming down the Return Road, this 1928 T35 Grand Prix Race Special (with an engine of 2.9litres from a T44) felt very evocative of an era.

Bob Mellors and bright blue comes around Pardon.

Chris Hudson rounds Pardon in a Type 35B blur of beige Bugatti!

Blue Bugatti, beret, and power on! BF 7717 gets going into Ettore's. You may gather that the driver is concentrating ...

Pilots get ready, awaiting the call down the paddock from the terrace.

Hastening away, BF 6015 gathers pace on leaving Prescott.

Edmund Burgess cuts through the Esses with a wheel up in his own style as the Type 51 lifts her undercart.

Opposite: Serious power. Tim Dutton brought the 4.9 Litre for display in 2017. One of just a few Type 54s so configured.

Travelling in style – an early Bugatti with lovely leather and cycle-wings and running boards.

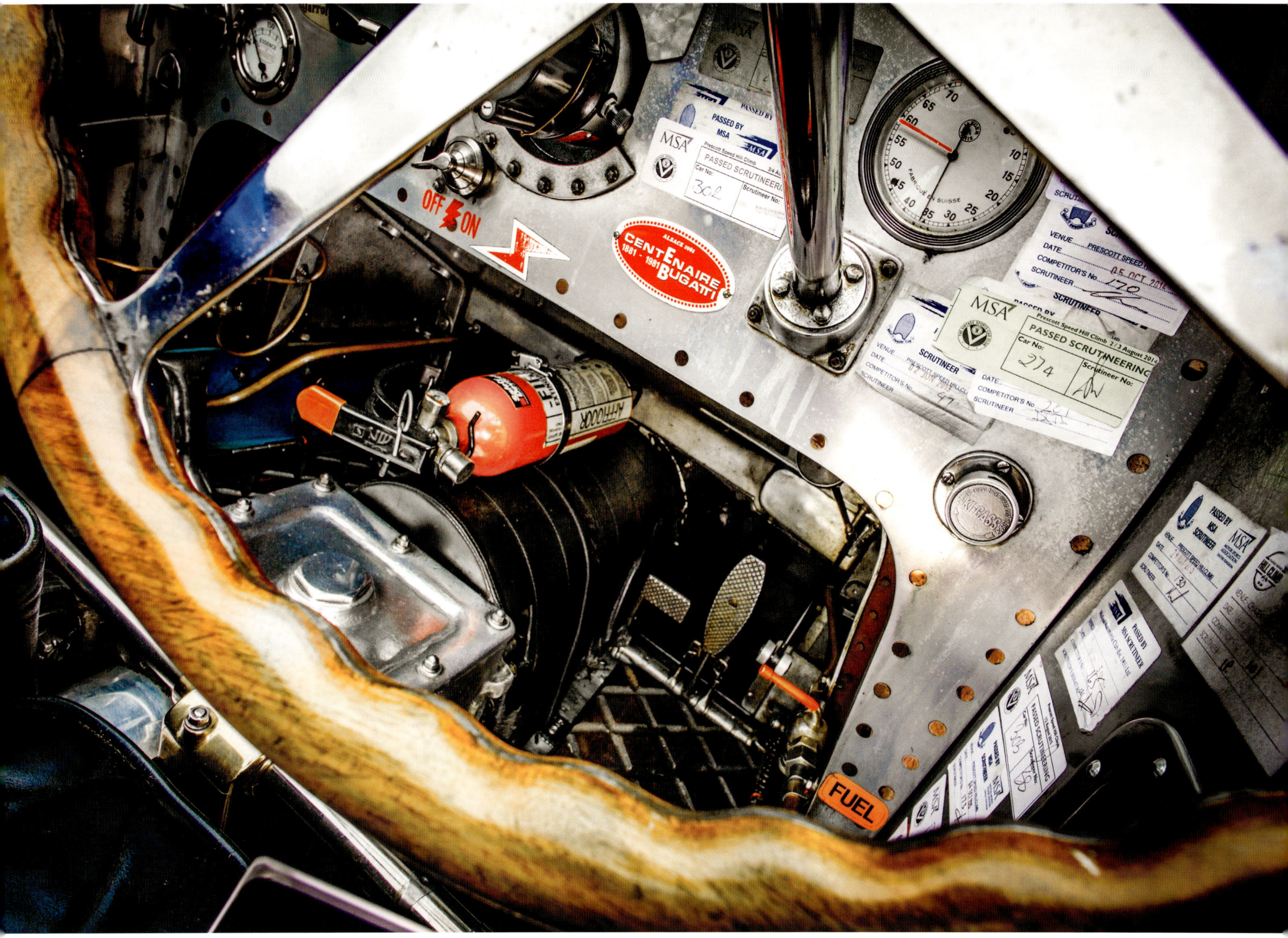

Inside the footwell of a 'working' Bugatti. It seems to have spent a lot of time at Prescott!

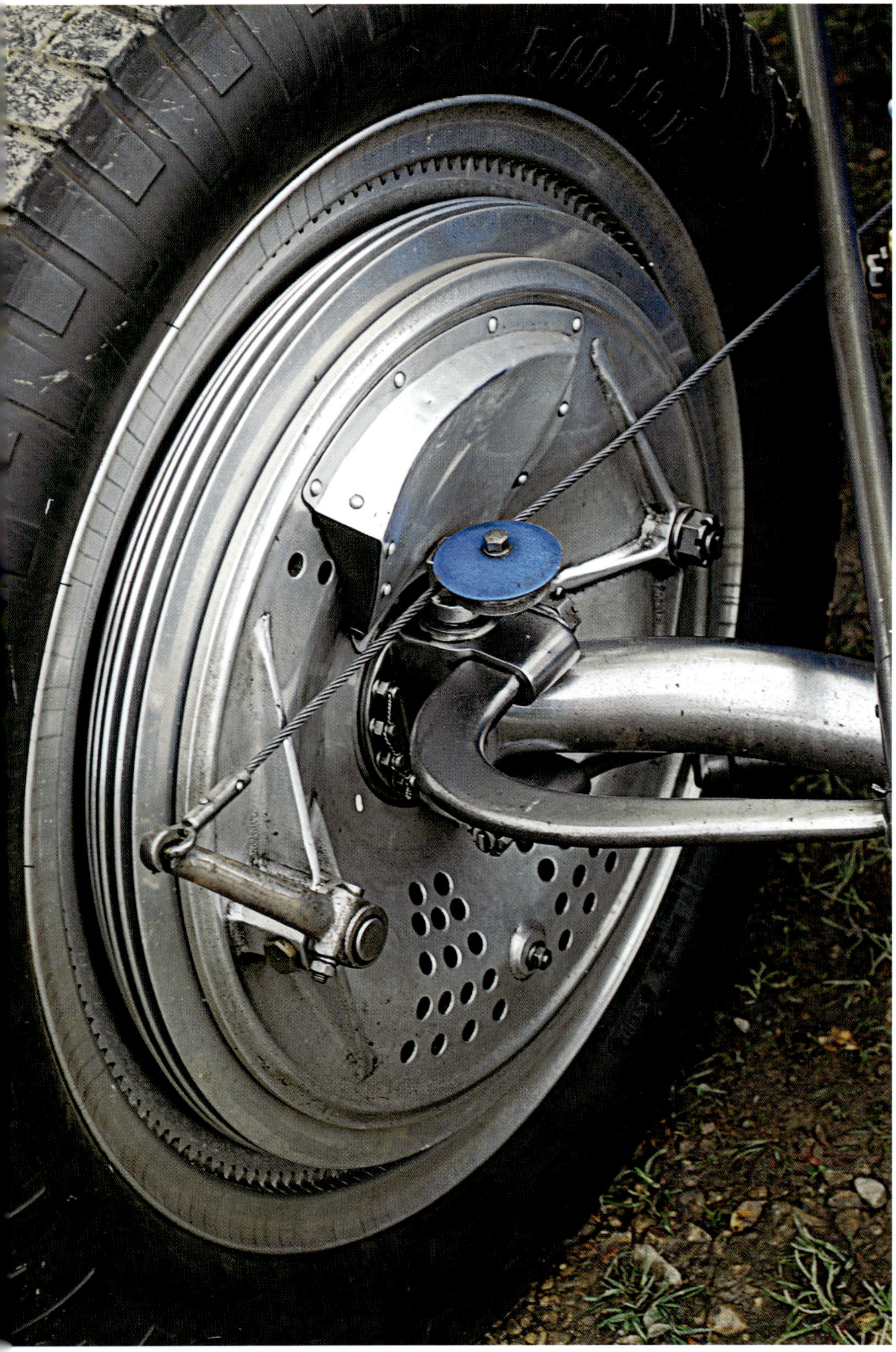

Ellipsoid Bugatti design perfection. A Type 57, and it's Parisian registered.

Brakes were always an issue for Bugattis. A switch to hydraulic actuation helped. This is the back of a T59 wire wheel and alloy disc combination load-bearing design.

Bright blue and dark blue as Bugatti blue catches the shadows up on the terrace as Type 59 and Type 22-series are caught in calm repose. The origins of the Type 59's shape stem from just a couple of years after the earlier car was new – a major leap in design language.

Stephen Gentry in the Type 35B speeds along with a passenger at Prescott.

Mr Tebbett goes up the hill in the Type 22 Sports Tourer in a blur of dark blue and brass.

Mike and his passenger glide into Prescott at the end of that young lad's first Bugatti ride.

Ettore's signature atop an engine. Roller-bearings, hand finished cranks, curved valve stems and valve guides, sculpted pistons, hollow axles, superb suspensions, and so much more came from the man.

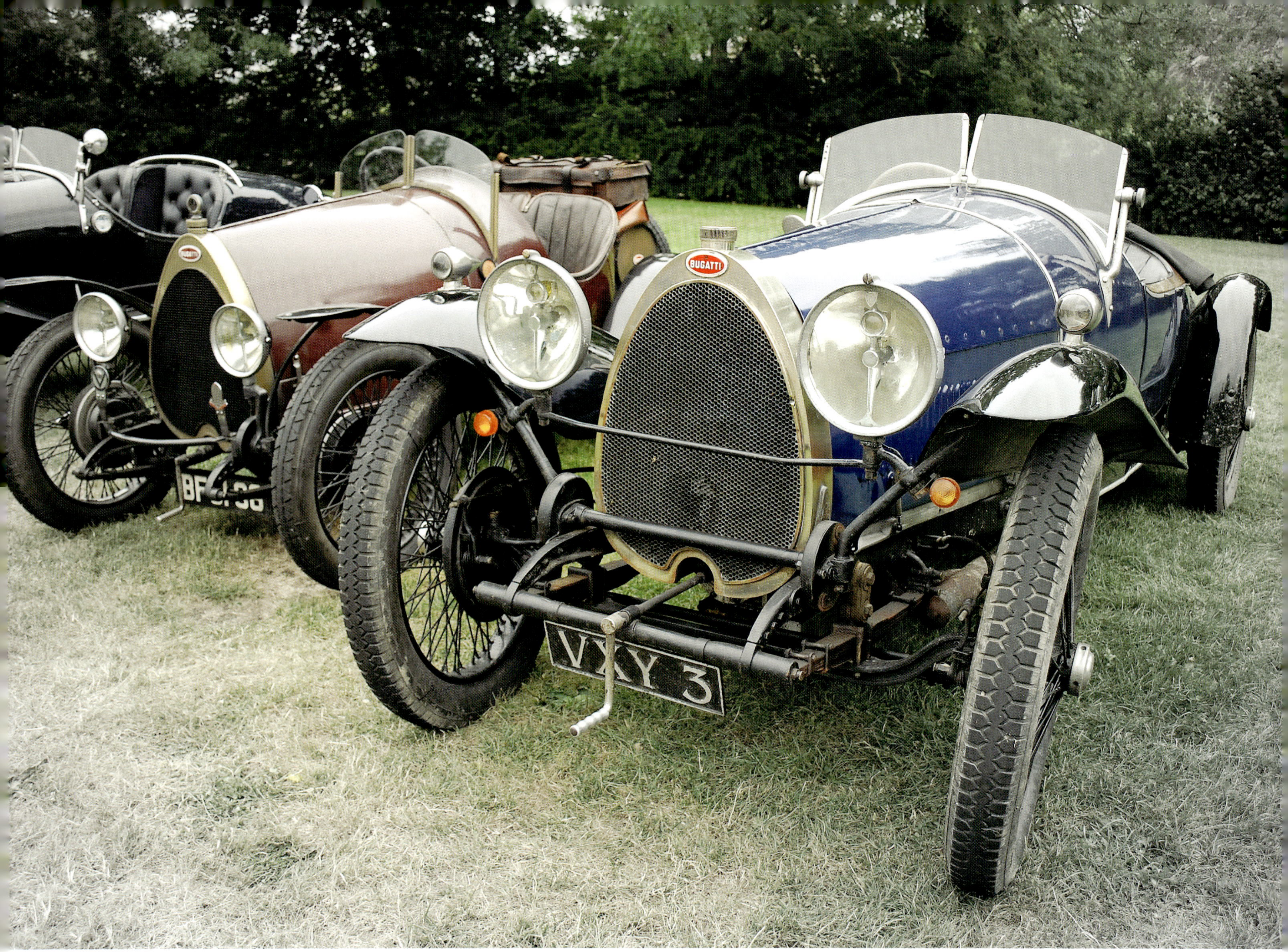

Bugatti 'faces' as Types 13-to-30 rest on the lawn with 'Tourer' elegance.

Simple but elegant.

It could have been decades ago, but it was in the twenty-first century. Mr Burgess goes up the hill in 'FHS'.

Bugatti Blue! The packed paddock of the Bugatti Owners' Club eighty years at Prescott seen framed across the cabin of the Kadoorie T57. The wonderful sight of fifty-three assorted Bugattis really made the day.

Boat-tailed beauty coming off the hill, driving through the gates of nostalgia.

The intricate details of Bugatti design are seen in this shot of the Type 54 front end.

The ex-K. Bear 1935 T57 Ventoux 3.3litre streamliner hastens up the hill in sheer Jean Bugatti-penned style et luxe, owned by Allan McNab.

Club Chairman Charles Trevelyan and his stunning dark blue T37 captured at pace on a hot day at Prescott.

CHAPTER 3

Bugatti Magic

Ettore Bugatti (1881-1947) and his son Jean (1909-1939) made just under 8,000 cars (7,800 say some). This may be low volume production in a global context, but in the setting of its time, it was a remarkable figure for what began as a one-man band and which often had scant resources yet went on to touch not just automotive design and history, but industrial design and a global movement. Few car makers have so cleverly crossed the road between racing car production and road car reality in the manner of Bugatti.

Bugatti is now seen in an essentially Franco-Italian context, yet Ettore's early steps were decidedly German orientated and, indeed, the white hue of the very early Bugatti competition cars was based on the German national racing colour.

Blue, bright Bugatti blue, was to come later, a hue whose vibrancy speaks volumes of the origins of Bugatti in the heat of northern Italy and southern France, a colour of the visual wavelength that somehow is so correct for Bugatti.

Ettore's father Carlo was a Milanese furniture designer and maker; he pioneered the use of exotic woods and new Art Nouveau forms or function across chairs, jewellery and many items. That Ettore, Jean and Rembrandt Bugatti should do likewise with other objects proves that a unique and rare gene raced through the Bugatti men and their consciousness. Unlike his father Carlo, Ettore was more mechanical – motor cars beckoned; like Carlo, Jean would also gravitate to Paris. Sadly, Carlo's other son, Rembrandt, took his own life before he had lived beyond three decades, a genius tormented by the depression that is a human factor yet one so often smothered by the conditioned thinking of 'society'. He died early but not before he too had cast down exquisite art – notably his animal sculptures – a rendition of which formed the 'elephant' radiator mascot for the later Bugatti Type 41.

We can only wonder as to the great designs that were left unseen by Rembrandt's death, not least as it was actually Rembrandt who had an interest in things mechanical as opposed to furniture or silversmithing (Ettore's initial interests), a fact of which few were aware. Might Rembrandt have created cars, or locomotives, or even aircraft if he had lived?

Surely it is true that the Bugatti family talent remains unequalled in terms of its technical and design innovation and ethos – a real design research thinking. Bugatti created a technical force and a 'design language' *long* before trendy modern designers tapped into the past, retro-pastiche, the 'designer graphic' or even into their own true original twentieth century designs.

The obvious shot, but one that cannot be dismissed. The badge that means so much.

Ettore started out with a passion for art, and then for motorcycles; Bugatti made contributions as an apprentice to Pruinetti & Stucchi for a light tricycle-type car, then in 1900 for ideas about four-wheeled cars that were initially realised in the form of a car design sponsored by benefactors in Milan. This was a small, four-wheeled light car or *voiturette* that won a prize at the Milan industrial exhibition of 1901. There followed a Bugatti relationship with the German de Dietrich and in 1904 a de Dietrich-Bugatti was reality

The famous front-wheel angle captured on full lock as 'CPW' gets going.

(also sold under licence as 'Burlington' in Britain). Ettore is said to have offered designs to the French at this time in a submission to Turcat-Méry, but which did not succeed. He continued to have German dealings then time working from Cologne/Koln with Deutz. He had also provided input to Mathis and to Hermes. Deutz gave Ettore their lead engineer's position when he was only twenty-three years old. This was a significant feat, not least as he was walking in the shoes of previous Deutz names such as Gottleib Daimler and of Wilhelm Maybach – serious 'names' of automotive achievement.

Ettore then set up in the often-fluid borderland of Franco-German Alsace, and had by 1909 produced his own 'homebuilt' car design – a 'Type 10'. He had already experimented with shaft-drive to replace the conventional thinking of chain-drive. It seems Ettore's mind never stopped thinking and his pencil was rarely still.

This period led to a contact with the Peugeot family that soon produced a 'Bugatti-ised' baby or Bébé Peugeot. Consulting to the French, at that time perhaps the fulcrum of the early car, led Ettore (and then his son Jean) to bigger and better things. This same period, *circa* 1910-1911, saw Ettore produce ideas at Molsheim, via financial backing from German investors including the de Vizcaya family. Now, Bugatti really was a car maker based in Alsace.

The true genesis of his own cars was the 1,327cc, Type 13, that had its roots in Ettore's thought first set down in Cologne as Mathis design thought and added to with Type 10 ingredients and Ettore's developing ideas. The new Bugatti car was a decidedly sporting car so different to the baby Peugeot that Bugatti authored at this time – although accounts differ as to which was born first. We might say that Peugeot contracted their light car's design concept from Ettore who already had it off the drawing board and into prototype stage. We should also recall that the Bébé Peugeot employed the reversed quarter-elliptic rear springs that became a Bugatti hallmark. Yet the Peugeot lacked thc Type 13's handling finesse. Today, you can see the Bébé Peugeot in action at Prescott alongside a Bugatti Type 13; says much for the sheer joy of the place, the BOC and the Bugatti Trust.

The First World War saw Ettore move to Paris – hence the consequent French connection and context of Bugatti cars. After the war and the Treaty of Versailles, Bugatti's old German home at Molsheim was now in France. So he returned to begin volume car production.

Did his wartime base in Paris, work in the aero industry and the presence of the likes of Gabriel Voisin and his advanced engineering and aerodynamic thinking inspire Ettore to his greater philosophy of engineering and design? Did Alphonse Penaud's designs make a mark upon Ettore's thoughts? What of Armand Deperdussin's works or Pierre Cayla's thoughts? Of Esnault-Pelterie's thinking? Did Jacques Gerin's stunning Aerodyne inspire Jean Bugatti? Did the men of the *École Nationale Superieure de l' Aeronautique et de Construction Mecanique* – the *'Sup-'Aero'* as France's greatest receptacle of aero-auto-mechanical thinking in Paris inspire Ettore? Surely, he must have been at least motivated by such an avant garde engineering environment? Some think that such rarely cited effects may well be relevant to Ettore's (and Jean's) ensuing genius of output.

But it was Bugatti's Type 13 that had been successful in motor races, notably the French Grand Prix (not the Vingt Quatre Heures du Le Mans) *prior* to the First World War. By 1921, Bugattis were being regularly campaigned in competitive events.

In 1922, an eight-cylinder Bugatti was reality and by 1923, Bugatti had even produced an 'aerodynamic' race-engineered car. We can argue that Gabriel Voisin and Andre Lefebvre designed sophisticated 'Laboratoire' cars and that their engineering was innovative, but the 1920s Bugattis made great marks and cast down the basis of a great marque. In the Type 35 of 1924, Ettore Bugatti married advanced chassis design and enhanced engine mechanicals to new coachwork forms that became a stepping stone to the 1930s and to Jean Bugatti's own 'game-changing'

Adam Ward's silver Type 40 zooms towards the camera in all its glory.

car designs that took huge strides for the motor car and for the driving of them by drivers.

The essential mid-1920s Type 35 brought a revolutionary new design and engineering language to sports racing cars. Un-supercharged, supercharged, a series of engine and chassis modifications, all led to the sporting tourers, the racing cars, and the grand Bugattis themselves. From hollow axles, curved inlet valves tracts, optimised cylinder head design, special wheel designs, and an early technique of adding lightness, Ettore thought about everything on his cars. Aerodynamics, suspension, body stiffness, expensive castings and extrusions, it was all here – even brakes that finally matched the performance! Remember, a true Bugatti racing engine could exceed 6,500 rpm without eating its crankshaft or shredding a 1:1/5 ratio supercharger. Just so long as the oil and fuel pressure pumps were kept hand-charged … No matter, Ettore had added an extra oil pump on the cambox to ensure camshaft lubrication, as early as 1913!

Jean Bugatti's cars of the 1930s invoked a hallmark of design that used raked, radically inclined windscreen forms, swept surfaces, two-tone graphics and design details applied to wheels, bumpers, grilles, interiors, trims, in fact the whole car was a 'holistic' design form. Underneath still lay Bugatti's intelligent suspension, chassis and engine ingredients. Through the handful of Type 41s, and on to the Atalante, Stelvio, Ventoux and Type 57 C teardrop, Jean created cars that became legends of design and of driving. We might suggest that as an act of *pur sang* purism, Jean's Type 59 racer of 1933 frames the ultimate function of the competition car of its era – and an influence that then cast its legend across decades of subsequent design.

The T59 or Type 59, in its handful of twin-cam, 2.8 and then 3.2 litre cars, took the art of the grand prix racer to new heights. Here was the 'spine' bodywork technique, wire wheels with a load bearing rim and backplate, and a long low stance that prefaced American 'low-riders' by years. Type 59 was packed with technical expertise that included a double-reduction gear rear axle configuration, advanced one-piece eight cylinder 'straight' block with integral head and inclined overhead valves, and the idea of a supercharger driven by a separate mechanism. A minimal frontal area and lightweight all added to the performance.

Perhaps the 1930s road-going and racing circuit output of Bugattism all became a bit elitist – a far cry from Ettore's early light or *voiturette*-related cars, yet this was the course of fate, fashion, and the fiscal needs of exquisite car making for a special clientele. A factory at Molsheim did not run on fresh air. Advanced design devoured money, and employees needed paying.

In the background, Ettore did more than dabble in boats, trains, aviation and Parisian life. As early as 1931, he also designed an electrically-powered child's car and Jean worked on an electric, 36 volt Type 56 city car and was thinking and sketching for the future. Yet post-war, by 1963, the 'original' Bugatti company was gone, and so too was Jean who had died in August 1939. Thankfully, through various modern era iterations of Artoli family effort, and Volkswagen AG enthusiasm, a modern varietal of Bugatti exists and it seems to have travelled through such delights as the perfectly sculpted EB110, the perhaps controversial Veyron, and now has reached dizzying heights in the new Chiron.

Yet herein, we are mainly concerned with pre-1939 Bugattis and their lives and functions on a British hillside and its ancient apple orchard amid a British

Bugatti men gather to talk – as they do!

obsession with all things Bugatti. Neither should we forget that the Bugattis themselves recognised the British Bugatti addiction – bringing the works team to Prescott with their blue transporters! What a sight. Jean Bugatti drove the hill, and the Bugattis gave the British Bugatti Owners Club a Bugatti. At a swish dinner at a London hotel in early 1939, Jean Bugatti (who would be dead within months) announced that Ettore had decided to donate a car for Club use at Prescott – not least for members who did not own a Bugatti to compete in. The car was a Type 51 and was factory black – soon changed to Bugatti blue! A black and yellow stripe was applied to mark the car and its Club colours. A fee of £5.00 was levied for any member who wanted to drive the car up the course in competition. A few members took a sedate drive, but a Richard Shakspeare drove it in anger at the Club's international meeting on 30 July 1939, but this was the only occasion that the car would compete – war clouds were gathering and the Club's events at Prescott were closed for the duration.

Brescia the Baby Bugatti

According to no lesser a scribe than the late 'Bill' Boddy, the little 'Brescia' Bugattis were the most exciting of the smaller vintage cars. If you go to Prescott and watch them haring up the hill, all fleet of foot, nimble and 'pointy' rather than raw and slithery like a supercharged Type 35, or Types 54 or 59, the cars' abilities are clear: other smaller light car types vie for traction on the hill, and even a lightweight Morgan will scrabble to fight off a Brescia barrel. For the Bugatti little tubbies are far more agile than they look. Double declutch, grab second gear, and that engine and its clever torque delivery will carry you away.

These small Bugattis have a strong following in Club circles and they seem to congregate together in a friendly little group at Prescott's 'Bugatti Park' top terrace where owners gather, talk of Brescia stuff, and fettle and fiddle their delightful little machines – fouled plugs and oiling issues being to the fore and often spilling onto the hallowed turf and tarmac of Prescott.

Originally conceived as early as 1910, the first small Bugatti cars had a square radiator. But soon the hallmark of the egg-shaped radiator grille gave way to a pear or teardrop-shaped radiator. The Type 13 gave rise to what became Bresicas, even though the cars existed before being retrospectively tagged as 'Brescia'. With a distinctive eight-valve (and latterly sixteen-valve) configurations and equipped with the reversed quarter elliptic springs, front half-elliptics, short chassis, and a host of Ettore's on-going engineering applications inside the engine block and, the soon to arrive 16 valve *multi-soupape*, 1,368cc specification, the small Bugattis became a real force to be reckoned with. As early as 1910, the eight valve cars were used in competitive events and by 1919 two were exhibited in London. They were to be cited as Type 13 and through the Type 20, as variations upon a purist's theme. Etttore raced the eight valve cars before and after the First World War – finally adding four wheel brakes to address the type's reluctance to deliver retardation – although at first they were an expensive £25.00 option! Sixteen-valve Type 13s formed a Bugatti racing team and found success at an early Le Mans in 1920 in the Voiturette Grand Prix.

But even the later small Bugatti cars have the roller-bearing crankshaft engine and steering box mounted on the crank arm – real 'designer' solutions. Much was refined and added, even at this stage of the marque's life.

After taking the top podium places in the 1921 Brescia Grand Prix (using slightly enlarged engines), and an average speed of 72 mph, the cars became known as the 'Brescia' Bugattis. The 16 valve (Brescia) Types 13, 22, and 23 offered displacements of 1,358, 1,453, 1,496 cc.

The driver de Vizcaya (one of the two de Vizcaya brothers and sons of Ettore's original backer) took his Brescia to 4th in class at the Isle of Man race in 1922. The British loved these baby Bugattis and the addition of twin-magnetos only added to the magic. A few of the Brescia were even licensed manufactured in Britain. All Brescias had a penchant for oiled-up plugs, temperamental gearboxes, and a general need for regular fettling, but it did not seem to put their pilots off. Names such as Rivers Fletcher, and Raymond

Chiron must be blue!

Mays (he owned a pair of the cars tuned up by pre-Bentley fame Amherst Villiers, 7,000 rpm being touted!) soon took these cars to their affections. A then unknown Major H. Segrave also bought a Brescia; Brooklands was a regular home to the 'baby Bugs' as they became known.

A Jarvis-bodied Brescia was also offered. A one-off long-chassis Brescia was built as a 'Brescia Modifee' Type 23 for British owner Leo d'Erlanger as late as 1925. Several 'Modifee' Bugattis were created in the early 1920s. Up to 1926, 2,000 of the Brescia varietals were manufactured. We should also cite 'Black Bess', latterly raced at Brooklands but originally delivered to aviator Roland Garros, as an exquisite car. Bugatti also experimented with a large, 5 litre-engined 'versions' of the short chassis type. Another Edwardian era, pre-war Type 18 was fitted with the 5 litre engine and driven by Ettore Bugatti, it was then purchased by Colonel Giles and in recent years was seen at Prescott driven by Nigel Arnold-Foster in 1979-1980 when it set a VS-CC Edwardian class record on the hill.

Today, it is Prescott that provides a British blur of the deceptively fast Brescias – of which nearly 2,000 were manufactured.

The former curator of the Bugatti Trust, Richard Day, built a Bugatti Type 22 from original parts upon a replica chassis and drove it at Prescott regularly. The car had an intriguing rear body configuration and was hand built using traditional methods. Hugh Conway did likewise with his building of a Type 35 'Bugatti' that hinted more at recreation than replica.

Bugatti would next produce its first sports tourers – enlarged cars such as Type 30, 38 and Type 40, 44 – all with longer chassis, more power (1,991cc and up to eight cylinders in twin four-cylinder blocks), overhead camshaft, and four seats. 1927 would see the 40 series debut and use of the 2,991cc engine. There followed the Types 30 and 40 series respectively. In these, Bugatti moved into two-seat and four-seat cars with more power, and more presence. So were the tourer and grand sport era cars of the mid-1920s and beyond. Monobloc, four-speeds, and accurate steering took these cars into rarefied driving territory. These cars rarely float and steer with direct accuracy – like most Bugattis. So were born the first upmarket Bugattis with the ability to be used as a family car, sporting tourer, or fast sprinter with one or two on board. Braking remained an issue – with the hydraulic, pump-the-pedal system being replaced by a mechanical cable actuation for better reliability. Bugattis now had front brakes! By 1927, the Tourers had been developed and refined. The three-litre Type 44 of 1928 reached new levels of refinement, power, and handling due to better weight distribution.

Type 35 – from *voiturette* to racer

After dabbling in the early aerodynamics or streamlining habit with the Type 30 2 litre with its conical, fluted exhaust-flowed tail and narrowed, faired in

Chiron coming off the hill for the first time: sheer style that finally seems to capture the magic of a Bugatti past. Surely Louis would approve?

Early Bugattis did not have the trademark radiator – even early Type 13 iterations.

frontal 'mouth', a radical Type 23 'Tank' was a car deliberately designed as a grand prix racer by Ettore with an early use of a one-piece 'pontoon' body (as was Gabriel Voisin's ideas). Yet this Bugatti was almost a step too far in design and body styling terms and was unsuccessful. So paradoxically, Ettore Bugatti took a step sideways and obliquely forwards in the design of his next racer – the Type 35. This provided a more marketable, more 'acceptable' body style with separate cycle-type wings, yet *did* offer a streamlined tail, and a lower, narrower grille with lesser frontal area in a new style – albeit perhaps making visual reference to a certain FIAT body design of 1923.

However, Ettore's sharp, lithe body styling, allied to advanced suspension, and an efficient engine, amid superbly responsive steering and handling in the new Type 35 of 1924, provided not just a design base plate, but also a stepping stone to the future as a combination of ellipsoid engineering form as function taken to the detailed exquisite as only Bugatti could.

Such wonderful details, such as the cast alloy wheels with the brake drum location cast integrally into the wheel's hub, can only be cited as design genius. The car's torque delivery was also absorbed by two externally mounted radius rods of just-thick-enough specification located at each rear side with ball pivots. The hollow-forged, one-piece front axle was utterly new in 1924: the forged 'eye' that encircled the slim leaf-spring also created a Bugatti design motif. Type 35 was also the first racing car to have a fully finished, plated and painted body. Only the non-synchromesh gearbox, externally-operated, reverse-throw long-arm gear leaver and resultant action, were of 'conventional' thinking.

The steering wheel design and dashboard presentation were also new motifs that, like so much of this car, reeked of 'design' – but not in an arty 'bling' way, but instead as acts of totally pure engineering excellence wrapped in one man's design purism that seems to have touched the hearts and minds of so many. A car that, as they say, 'set the standard' for Bugatti design for years to come.

From the original 'Tipo 35' came much larger-engined versions, supercharging, and the Types 35A 2.3 litres, 35C (2 litres), 37, 39 (1.5 litre but 8 cylinders), 40 and Type 50 series derivations. These used engines of 2.3, 2.8, 3.3 litres (dry sump spec) and ultimately 4.9 litres (supercharged).

So came the 'Grand Prix' Bugatti – the Type 35, Type 35T, Type 39, with engines ranging from 1,991cc and 2,262cc. At least 100bhp was delivered, with up to 150bhp when supercharged (Type 35B): 130mph/200Km/h was on hand, complemented by an amazing soundtrack. The hand machined crank was made with hardened-steel alloy machined to forensic detail and with reliable lubrication. Like so much of the detailing of the Type 35 baseplate design and its derivatives, this was true Bugattism. Above all perhaps, there was that body, that amazing shape that really was a new design language.

In the Type 54, Bugatti engineering would deliver 4.9 litres with 300bhp and led even the likes of Phil Hill, the grand prix Formula One driver, to describe this chassis/engine combination as the 'scariest' car he had ever driven.

The 'face' of an early Bugatti is surely evocative. This one was captured on the Return Road.

In the 1970s era at Prescott, the Type 35B formerly owned by Eddie Grenall in the 1950s, was a regular sight. The car was restored by Geoffrey St John, being used by him from 1963 to 1972 prior to a change of ownership to Ian Preston who campaigned the car at Prescott, prior to Terry Cardy's ownership and then sale to U.S. residency.

The combination of the earlier Type 40's 1½ litre engine, placed into the optimised grand prix chassis, also created the Type 37.

Type 51/A at 2.3 litres brought twin-cam power delivery, and the two, four wheel-drive Type 53s built were an early form of all-wheel traction (twin rear wheels also being tried) and Jean Bugatti brought his Type 53 to Prescott. Although ideal for hill climbs in tractive terms, the car had questionable steering characteristics and a long wheelbase; Jean crashed at Shelsley Walsh with the handling being the issue – not the driver. Barrie Price, the one-time BOC chairman who had owned and driven all but one of the Bugatti cars since the 1950s, would drive Uwe Hucke's Type 53 in the rain at Prescott in August 1985 and set a time of 51.70 on the short (original) course in the rain. This was the car's first competitive British event in over 50 years and spoke volumes for Price's abilities in what was, dare we say it, a bit of a long wheelbase yacht of a Bugatti!

If a Type 57S was a big-car handful on Prescott's narrow track and tight bends, then ultimately, there came the 3.2 litre Type 59 – more of a 'muscle car' and lowered too, but a Bugatti that combined a lithe body with real grunt; in a way it was a 'hot rod' of a Bugatti. Yet this car retained traditional cable operated brakes and legacy fittings. The clock, or should we call it a chronometer, remained large on the dashboard – almost as important as a speedometer to a Bugatti driver!

No longer were Bugattis light cars of *voiturette* descent; Bugattis were now larger, heavier (but still nimble) and true racers. Today, Rupert Marks' 1934 Type 59 resides inside the Bugatti Trust when at rest, but it makes a stunning sight and sound on the hill during its regular outings, scything up the hill in a wail of Bugatti blue as an example of ultimate design. John Marks had previously campaigned the Type 59 (built upon original frame number 8, with subsequent parts) at Prescott in the 1980s era, taking the cross-over course record in 1989 at a time of 57.43 seconds. John Marks, who had owned a trio of Bugattis, joined the board of the Bugatti Trust in 1990; he also held high office in the BOC.

Tim Dutton brought the rare Type 54 (in a rare pale blue hue) with the enlarged 4,972cc engine to Prescott in 2017 and alongside Stephen Gentry's similarly hued 2,300cc Type 35B. Stephen has been campaigning Bugattis at Prescott for years (and running Gentry Restorations Ltd) and supplies those lovely Bugatti protective over-blankets that keep a Bug safe and warm.

Sun, spray, and light cascade down onto the Bugatti blue. It's 'CPW' again – up close and personal as only Prescott seems to deliver.

In 2017 at Prescott we saw the new Chiron parked beside its ancestors. Never did genealogy tempt so much and dare to deliver. Purists might (understandably) inhabit the Bugattism of the past, but we can surely celebrate the shock of the new. Thanks to the Bugatti Owners Club, and to the Bugatti Trust, a great story, a legacy, is safe. In 2018, the Club celebrated its 80th anniversary. There must be many ghosts upon Prescott's tarmac, or resting under its apple trees.

Ultimately, the old Bugatti and the new Bugatti inhabit and inherit Prescott and its Bugatti Owners Club. From pre-First World War days to the heyday of Bugatti, across the Prescott years to the 80th anniversary and beyond, from the latest Chiron to whatever lies ahead, here can be found the soul of a glorious past amid the afterwards and the before of something truly special.

Shot from the terrace banking, the 'cycle-type' wings add a different air to the elliptical form.

So lies the Bugatti legend in Britain, its blue, and Prescott's timeless appeal. The place and its people are a privilege to have known. After a day here, you can close your eyes and still see searing flashes of bright blue, still smell the burned fuel, still hear the whine and the wail of Bugattis attacking the hill. It has ever been so at Prescott, and always will be.

Elegance captured. Simple but effective as the classic time-warp repose. Was this 2017 or decades earlier? Bugatti design never ages, is never a retro-pastiche, it is timeless and beyond fashion.

The plate that says it all – in unrestored glory.

Classic line-up as Type 40 and siblings get ready to go. Is that a factory-body on the Type 40? Some may think so, others still hunt for its origins.

Above and overleaf: The very rare, British, Jarvis & Sons Ltd of Wimbledon-bodied car, looks good in this mid-blue hue – the Dewhurst's Type 40 always attracts interest.

COACHWORK
DESIGNED
& BUILT BY
JARVIS & SONS, LTD.
WIMBLEDON
S.W. 19.
PHONE 2820

It's that man again. Prescott moments as Julian Eckersley and car await the next 'go'.

The Bugatti Trust was formed in 1987 by the late Hugh G. Conway. It is now probably the world's leading centre of excellence for specific Bugatti research, design thinking and exhibitions. It is not on a Californian museum scale and was not meant to be. The Trust was financed partly through the selling of the Type 35C GNE 801 – the 'Genie' by Alan Howarth – raising £350,000.

The Bugattitstes come down the hill return road in a classic convoy amid a stream of Bugatti blue.

The Prescott Paddock seen on a busy day from the business end of Bugatti.

Type 13s really are quick and this one was captured at full chat going from Pardon to the Esses.

John Huntley in the 1925 Type 30 captured from above as he accelerates from the Start.

The lawn at the Bugatti Trust makes an excellent exhibition area. Here, a gaggle of sport and tourer types take rest under the trees. The green 1927 T37A has that wonderful aura of authenticity to the fore.

Josh Read at the wheel of the Trevelyan T37, 'SY6'. Hopefully this young man will be inspired to Bugattism in years to come, after such a formative experience.

Bonnets up on Bugatti Terrace – a 1926 factory works Bugatti on 'race' tyres (pale blue), the famous 'Genie' (red), and the chairman's steed (dark blue).

Really bright blue as Mike Ward's Type 13 barrels along with panache. Still a light car or *voiturette* type car, yet one that goes with gusto – if a little harder to stop... Oh, and do hand pump the oil and fuel pressures up before you leave!

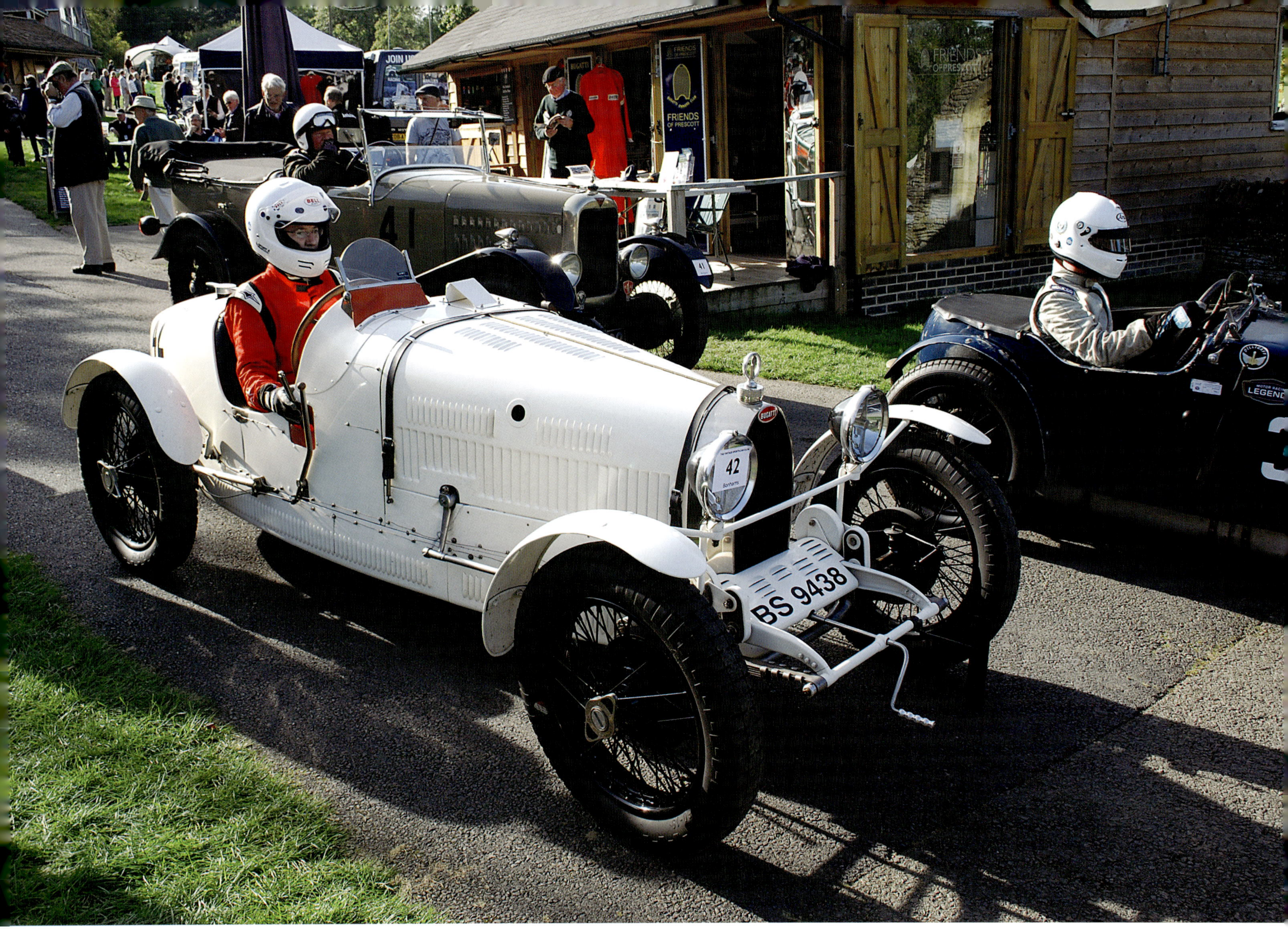

Afternoon delight as Jane Murray in BS 9438 lines up. Such access and such atmosphere are what makes Prescott so good.

Tony and Christine Rippon with their delightful 1925 Type 23 Brescia in blue – Tony having purchased the car in 1954, and subsequently risen to the rank of Bugatti Owners Club President. Tony has inspired many a Bugattiste and also penned his superb Bugatti memoir *Sixty Shades of Blue*. His wife and children have all supped at the grail of Bugatti driving and ownership and like other 'names' of Bugatti ownership, they are part of the Prescott legend.

Waiting for the off, engine burbling away, tension mounting.

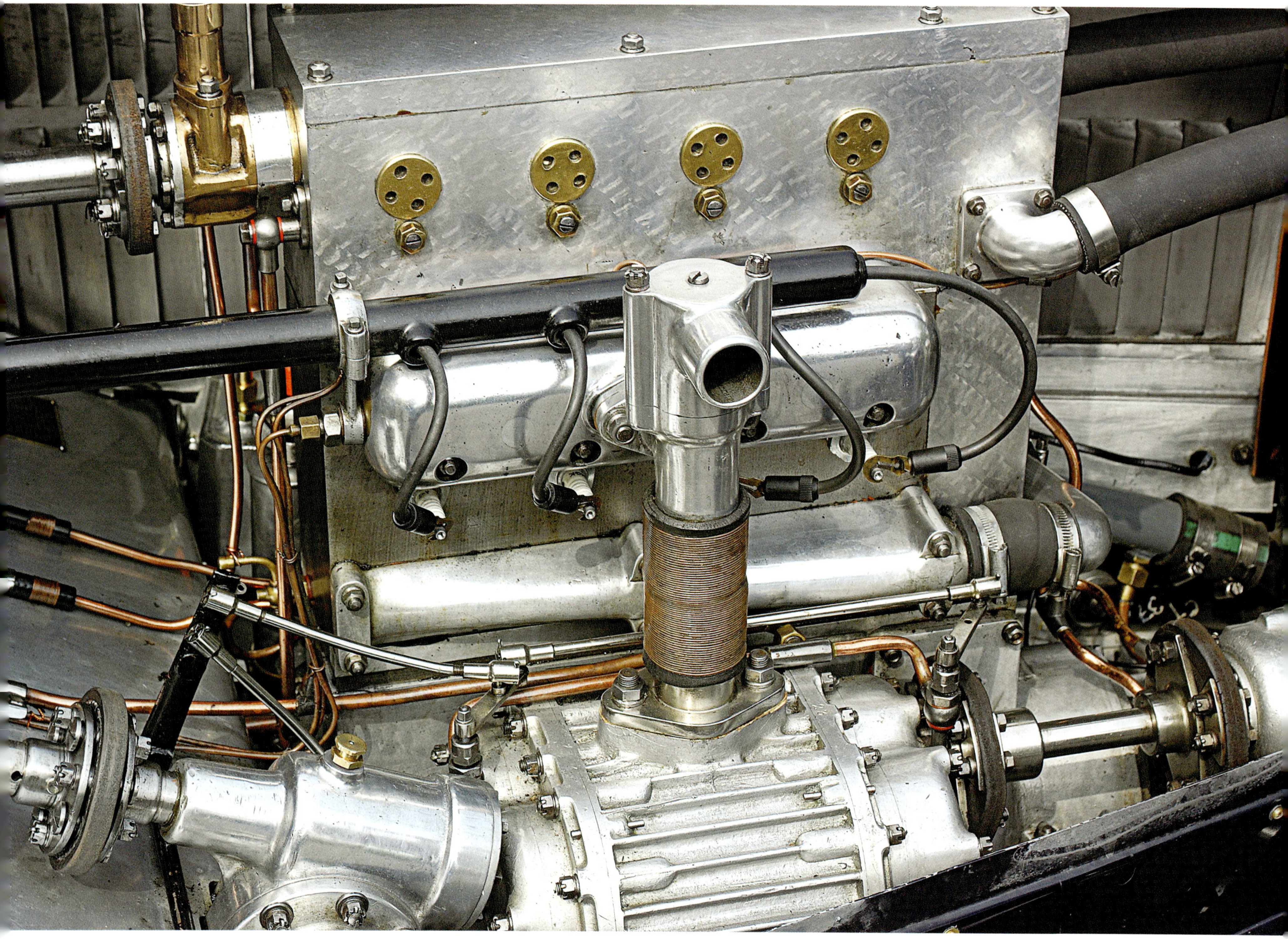

Bugatti sculpture in steel. The lightly supercharged engine of the Trevelyan car.

CHAPTER 4

Vintage Delights

If you camp at Prescott, you will wake up, as I so often have, on a summer's morning as the dawn chorus gets going and the sky lightens to a pale blue tinged with pink then goes gold. As you stick your head out of your tent, caravan, motorhome, or the back of a van, Prescott eases into another hot day on the hillside. An early breakfast and a walk over to the paddock will reveal the ranks of Bugattis also awaking from their slumbers, or on VS-CC days, breakfast will unveil a plethora of wonderful old metal resting, but ready for mechanical momentum.

Soft early morning light will fall upon polished metal and that vibrant hue of bright Bugatti blue. Slashes of golden sunlight will bounce off the dark blue and the black painted cars. Silver cars will also shimmer as the day begins, birds rise and the smell of sizzling bacon seeps across the Orchard and the overflow fields. Get up really early and you can see the cars awake and then take a breakfast on the Clubhouse terrace.

La Vie en Blue? Bugatti Day? The Cotswold Trial? Or the VS-CC's main gathering? Well, some people inhabit only one camp, but many of us have a foot in more than one tribe or clan gathering. Even the occasional deluge and flooded tent cannot put people off staying at Prescott for a big two-day event. Cars and their owners arrive from all over the world to be part of these very special days. As so much changes in the world and in society, the fact that you can come here and live out the past in a modern context means a great deal.

Not everyone can afford a Bugatti, or a Delage, or real Riley, or a vintage beastie with which to tackle Prescott or attend the ranks of classic cars that line up in the Orchard. Yet non-vintage car owning enthusiasts are welcomed into the BOC and VS-CC fraternity with friendship and access to the real action. In this paddock there are no roped-off areas of elitist enclaves: long may it stay that way.

Vintage days at Prescott offer the pre-war car enthusiast a panoply of marques to feast upon. Of all, the main, annual August gathering, the VS-CC weekend Hill Climb meeting is, quite simply, the jewel in the crown. People fly in from the other side of the world to sup at this wonderful brew.

Up in the Paddock, ready for the hill, can be found everything from an early Mercedes to a Vale Special. The range of types on offer is truly outstanding: Austin Sevens, Bentley, ERA, Riley, Jaguar, Lancia, Alvis, Rover, Vauxhall, Delage, Frazer Nash, MG, GN; in fact, pick a name, it is likely to be there. Down in the Orchard, we find an equally stunning array of non-competing cars, and stalwarts of what we must correctly label, the Vintage Sports-Car Club – with the hyphen included please! And watch out for the VS-CC's Editor of the *Bulletin*!

The VS-CC is an interesting organisation inhabited by interesting people. Some are 'of an age' a bit like their cars, others are younger. Many of the members have supported the VS-CC for decades and refute the suggestion that they are eccentric, as some outsiders might (erroneously) perceive. Those in the know realise that this wonderful club is, like the Bugatti Owners Club, a collection of differing types of people who, whatever their varying tastes, are just like their cars – very interesting indeed. These people and their club are truly international in the appreciation of the cars and the driving of an era that has passed, yet was the most important epoch of the car and the magic of man's motoring.

The VS-CC has as part of its ethos a less moneyed attitude than some early car clubs of upper crust aspiration. So a variety of types of cars and their owners have always populated its numbers. Membership approaches 10,000 across the globe. The 'Pre-war car' movement provides the perfect VS-CC vehicle. Many Bugatti Owners Club members enjoy not just VS-CC membership but also play a role in VS-CC life. We might call it a cross-contamination of the classic car addiction.

Whichever the club, come rain or shine, Prescott is vintage (and veteran), classic car heaven, a world class collection of sights, sounds, action and all under open access with no VIP enclosures. Long may this superb experience continue and be protected from flash people and flash prices. How good it is to see the past racing towards us beyond the gates of remembrance in a blur of blue.

Words become superfluous, vintage imagery is the thing, so this narrative stops here and transfers you to the pictures that follow.

Chris Pring's ex-Desmond Titterington Allard J2 storms at the camera with true Allard impact. This car, once a star of the Festival of Britain, has returned from life in India and is the subject of much affection and an expert fettling.

Roland Duce and passenger in a lovely 1930s Alfa Romeo leaving Prescott. Alfas provided Bugattis with real competition on road and track.

Lagonda on the hill top with the Cotwolds behind. It may be large, but the Lagonda was, shall we say, quite effective (a 1935 Le Mans win proving the point). This is a quintessential Prescott paddock moment captured.

Bedelia – they are a sort of motorised bedlam. A coffin on wheels say some; huge fun say others – and the essential epoch of the light car *voiturette*; chain driven and painted in a certain blue.Mike Bullet is the Bedelia man to go to,here he is with hatted accomplice amid the Orchard.

Tom Hardman 'the vintage and classic car dealer' is a key spoke in the vintage movement's wheel and a VS-CC sponsor as principal associate. Tom has had an Austin Seven, and a Frazer Nash in his past. Here he is in his rare 1930s MG streamliner at high speed into the Esses. Note the twin rear wheel set up – as tried with Bugatti and the Steyr Allard at Prescott in decades past.

Light car lawn. An Amilcar and the related Vernon Derby frame a lovely line up. Often called the poor-man's Bugatti, Amilcar needs to be seen in its own wonderful light. Salomon and Moyet made light cars that became delightful cars – Amilcars. There was even a straight-eight powered Amilcar, but the supercharged 1100cc six-cylinder (roller-bearing) engined 1920s Amilcars represent something special of the belle epoch.

Amilcar roadster and coupé light cars – both in from Germany and idling away their time on the Prescott lawn – sheer vintage delight.

Page 149–153: This lovely Amilcar in French blue really has found a place in peoples' hearts. UC 53 'the Ian Patton/Terry McGrath car' is seen in action at Prescott. Such cars can still be purchased for 'normal' money. Utter delight.

73
UC 53

THE VINTAGE SPORTS-CAR CLUB
159
Bonhams
AMILCAR
BELL

759

COMP. No.
159
Bonhams
161
AMILCAR
UC 53

Amilcar fettling – close to the action.

The FIAT S76 – 'Beast of Turin' and campaigned by Bugatti driver Duncan Pittaway. It makes a big impact going up Prescott. Duncan drove it from Bristol to Goodwood on the motorway – stopping seven times to refuel and causing delight at the service stations!

The Swift Anzani with a vee-twin added to a Swift chassis. It goes – as the driver's face shows!

1950s Gilera twins: sheer delight as personal transport to Prescott. Pure class on two wheels.

Above and opposite: Changing the numbers the easy way – take a pen to your early motoring device. Mr Hickling is a VS-CC stalwart and so is his 1911 Sunbeam. Wicker-work seats seem so fitting.

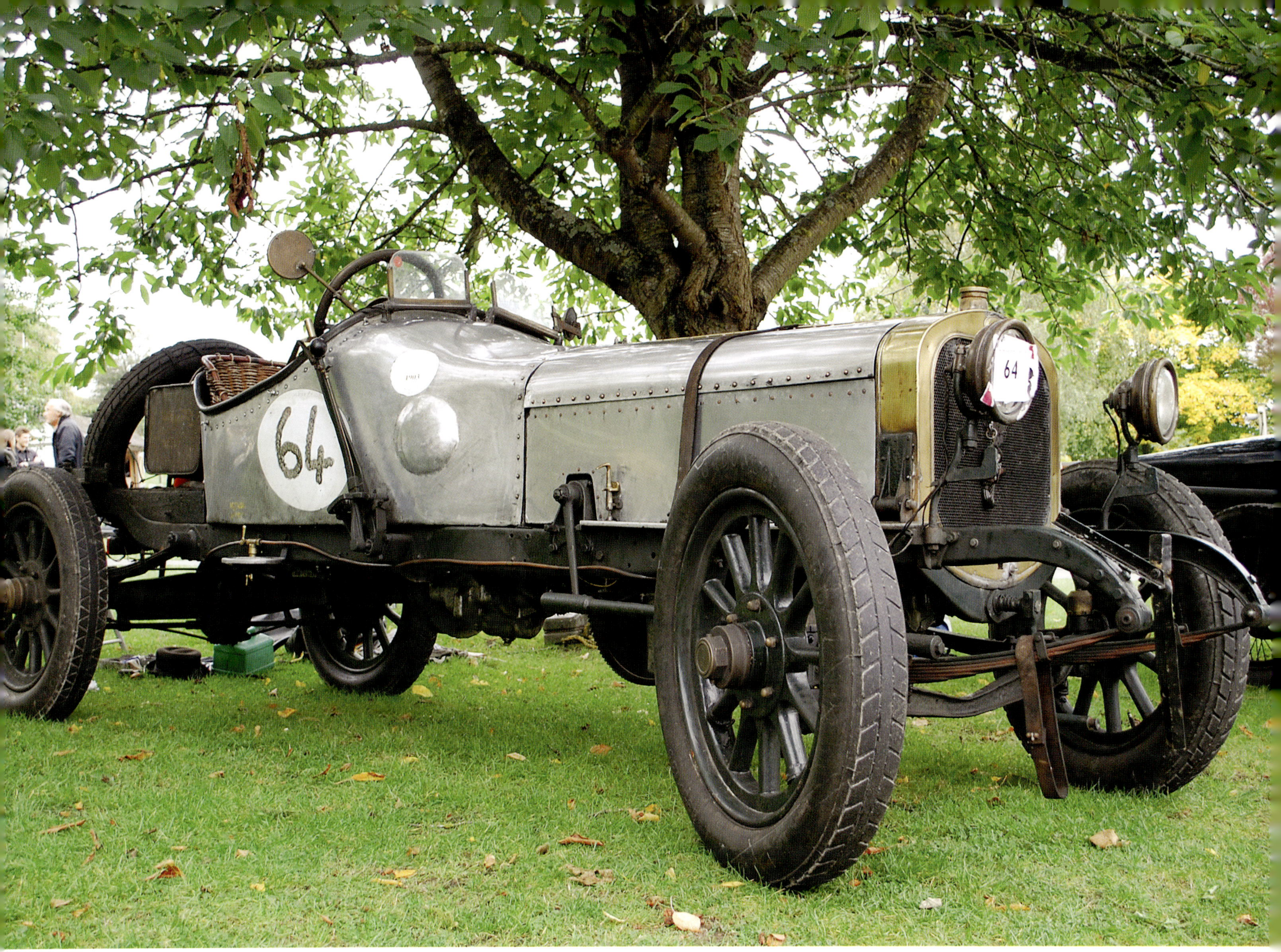
64
64

Salmson GS8 of Nicholas Williams shows off the badge, the blue, the moment. The Societé des Moteurs Salmson was an aero-engine maker, and produced licence-built GN cars before producing its own cars from 1921. The company died in 1953. Many people feel its 1920s and 1930s output under engineer Monsieur Petit was its heyday.

Frazer-Nash BMW 319 in GWR colours at Prescott where it is a regular delight.

Roland Duce arrives in the 1913 Vauxhall Prince Henry – just another addictive day at Prescott...

It's a rather rare 1933 Frazer-Nash Colmore and this is how to arrive at Prescott in VS-CC style – dignified taste!

Above and overleaf: Silverfish, the Morgan three-wheeler, scuttles up Prescott like a frightened insect.

127

Amilcar, blue, the Tricolor and chevrons – classic Prescott life in blue.

One for the Alfisti, Edward Williams in the 1933 Alfa Romeo Tipo B/P3 surges up the hill in 46.54 seconds.

Did a humble steering wheel ever look so good? So much thought went into Bugatti design.

Above and below: The Delage DM Sport of Hugh McGarel-Groves gets in on the action and then rests from its toils.

1930s Alfa Romeo streamliner rolls out of the Orchard with a young enthusiast making the most of the moment from the passenger seat.

It is a Delahaye 135M it is blue and powering up Prescott out of Pardon. So, life is good.

Roger Collings, past-President VS-CC and the 1903 Mercedes 60hp chain drive, with a newspaper to read amid the bustle of the Prescott paddock. As you do Sir! Oh and the rest of the family campaign in Bentleys. As you do...

On the Prescott hill – heading up towards the Esses as seen through the windscreen of a 1927 French car – the Chenard et Walcker, Berline: Nostalgia lives.

Roger Hayes in the superb Hayes family Allard J2. Roger is a Bugatti restorer of renown, having worked for Ivan Dutton Ltd for many years. He has fettled a string of Allards.

Above and overleaf: The 1912 Talbot 12hp goes up the Esses in fine style and with plenty of torque on offer. Then it returns.

61

Modern Morgan moments. Three-wheelers across the decades of Morgan captured as they head off for the Start at Prescott.

Mac Hulbert and his Alvis. This is what Prescott life is all about – fettling a real car with atmosphere to match. The famous red triangle badge means Alvis – but this one is not a tank – it's a 'Silver Eagle' Special of somewhat ERA-esque appearence. As Sir Douglas Bader used to say of his Alvis as he pulled out to overtake: 'make way for quality'.

Riley Ulster Imp. Once, Riley's were truly great sporting cars at the top of their class – and BMW had yet to make its mark on the sector. This is real British motoring heritage in blue and a privilege to witness. Today, Riley remains a (thankfully) dormant badge in BMW's hands...

Mike Read in his 1914 Chater Lea Singer Special with the Lionel Martin-tuned engine (Buff Form to match). Just taking in the atmosphere is what it is all about.

Klaus-Peter Mutschler and his family – the 1932 Alvis Speed 20SA is included in that. They drove from Germany to saviour the main VS-CC event of the summer. As Klaus-Peter says: 'Nowhere else in the world provides this'.

David Biggins in the 1913 'Rennwagen' makes a Mercedes arrival. Maybe we do not actually need to say anything as the moment speaks for itself.

Exquisite Edwardian era design – but from Paris. The literal translation of the makers script is 'refridgerator cloisonne' – but nothing Japanese is obvious...

A Delage and a hammer. The Longstone Tyres mobile pit helps out with a problem.

Bugatti talk. Rob Lamplough, racing driver, pilot, and more recently, a Bugatti owner. Club members chat as 'Robs' prepares for the off in his blue Bugatti – a real 'burbler'.

The legend of the name in alloy. Bugatti design at its exquisite detailing: gearbox casing on a Brescia. Don't forget to add oil!

MG Monthlery Midget moment as the blue magic arrives for another great vintage VS-CC day in a blue blur of 746cc supercharged joy! Pottering along we might say...

'Miss Bacfire' gets a push in the paddock, as she often does.

Asleep at Prescott! Driving is tiring. Nice hat. Great cars.

Chevrons after lunch. A very authentic looking Citroën Traction Avant slumbers on a Prescott afternoon, just because it can.

Rileys ready to go at 11.00AM on a busy Prescott morning. It proves that nostalgia is better than it used to be.

Rupert's Type 59 makes its mark as it burbles away from the camera.

Bibliography

Reference materials and communications

BUGATTI OWNERS CLUB et al. *Bugattis At Prescott*. Prescott 2007.
CONWAY, H.G. *Bugatti* Great Marques Series. Octopus Books Ltd. London 1984.
WOOD, J. *Bugatti: The Man and the Marque*. The Crowood Press. Ramsbury 1992.

The Bugatti Owners Club.
The Bugatti Trust.
The Automobile.
Bugantics.
Classic Cars.
Paul Gibbons, Archivist, BOC.
Angela Hucke, Curator, The Bugatti Trust.
BOC members.

Photographic Credits
Principal photography: Lance Cole.
Additional photographs:
Tim Read.
The Bugatti Owners Club (Archive).

Index